Think Upside Down
and
Live Life Fully

Marie-Anne Rasé

Editor - Jane Whiting

Grosvenor House
Publishing Limited

The right of Marie-Anne Rasé to be identified as the author of this
work has been asserted in accordance with Section 78
of the Copyright, Designs and Patents Act 1988

The book cover picture is copyright to Marie-Anne Rasé
Book cover designer - Roshan Rotzz

This book is published by
Grosvenor House Publishing Ltd
28-30 High Street, Guildford, Surrey, GU1 3EL.
www.grosvenorhousepublishing.co.uk

A CIP record for this book
is available from the British Library

ISBN 978-1-78623-001-0

TABLE OF CONTENTS

FOREWORD...v

DEDICATION..vii

PREFACE..ix

INTRODUCTION / THE BEGINNING.............................xiii

The start of the journey

IDENTITY 1

Who I am

BOUNDARIES 9

Space clarity

EXPECTATIONS 13

My expectations of others 13

My expectations of self..16

Others' expectation of me 17

GOAL SETTINGS 19

Aim, shoot, goal!

RELIGION & SPIRITUALITY..24

The seen and unseen

TRUE LOVE 29

Unconditional... really?

STAND OUT 33

Know the rules

JUDGMENT / GUILT / REGRETS..38

Your business is my business

AU NATUREL 43

Close to Mother Nature

 Food 43

 Skin 45

 Hair 45

 Health 47

 Exercise 48

CONGRUENCE 50

True to myself

WRAPPING UP 53

My final words (… for now)

FREEDOM OF SPEECH 56

How others perceive me (un-edited)

REACHING YOUR FULFILLED
SELF - PULL OUT SECTION 72

10 Most Significant Tips

ACKNOWLEDGEMENT 89

ANOTHER DEDICATION 91

ABOUT THE AUTHOR 92

WHERE AND HOW TO CONTACT ME 94

PUBLISHED BOOKS BY THE AUTHOR 94

 The Role of the Business Analyst Demystified

 Le rôle de l'analyste d'affaires démystifié

FUTURE BOOK COMING SOON 94

 The Beginner's Guide to Food Allergy & Intolerance

 (co-authored with Rebekha Gooden)

Foreword

There are, as we all know, more and more self-help books coming on to the market every day, written from all points of view and perspectives.

And yes, here apparently is yet another! So what makes this book different, special? Well the answer to that is simple - this book is different because its author is different!

Marie-Anne Rasé originally came to our Trainings a couple of years ago, and the first thing we noticed was her energy and enthusiasm for life, learning, and specially learning about herself, and learning from her own life.

She is what we call an 'experience sponge'....she soaks up as much as possible, and then lets it trickle out where it's most useful!

So with this book, Marie-Anne is letting you feel the benefits of every squeeze of that experience and wisdom sponge!

And because she is what is known as a Mismatcher, someone who likes to do things differently from others, she has always taken learnings from other people, honoured their opinions - and then made it her own, putting her own twist on things to make it all fit and work with her own values and beliefs.

So we very much recommend that you do the same thing with this book........take on board Marie-Anne's considerable learning from her own experiences, because she is wonderfully informative and knowledgeable........... but then make it your own, just as she does.

Because information and knowledge only become wisdom when we get them 'into the muscle', really make them part of ourselves.

That is the gift from Marie-Anne to you within these pages.

So read, learn, inwardly digest.............and most of all, enjoy!

Dee Shipman & Paul Jacobs
New Oceans Training & Coaching Academy
2016

Dedication

Dedicated to

My son Reuben
My daughter Rebekha
My daughter Jasmine
My grand-daughter Ly'ora

and

My future grand-children…

In lieu of an auto-biography, may this book give you an insight of
my journey towards the time when you were born; and may it
serve as an inspiration for you to reach your fulfilled self.

Amour, toujours
Mummy & Gammie

Preface

I first came across this quote last year in one of the NLP (Neuro Linguistic Programming) courses I was attending. It sounded incredibly simple, and I became so fascinated by this concept that I made a couple of changes straight after the course. I certainly got a result that I was not getting before! Making changes can be challenging. Introduce a new habit or pattern and soon our being will spring back to its previous comforting habit. My experience of people around me is that many of us get stuck in our usual habits, our usual thoughts, our usual behaviour...

I started writing this book on my last birthday November 2015. For many people, a birthday is a time of reflection and self-scrutiny. For me, that particular birthday brought forth a strong urge to 'bare it all' and to use my life experiences as a spring board for others to break the cycle of "If you always do what you've always done, you'll always get what you've always got."

The title "Think Upside Down" can be actually taken literally. What if we take a different physical position when we problem solve? What would happen? Would our mindset shift depending on the position? In trying to get the best photo shoot for the book cover that fitted with the title, I did a head stand. Truly! I nearly broke my neck along the way but one thing I can tell you is my thoughts were totally different for the few seconds that I managed to stay upside down with my head on a pillow and my legs propped up vertically against the wall. I am not recommending that you do a head stand; maybe you can try a different pose than the one you usually take when you are solving something. Being upside down, for one thing, gives whatever is in your sight a different angle and so you see it differently. This book challenges you to look at things from a different perspective; to challenge the status quo and the general and common behaviour/habits and beliefs so you can rid yourself of the unnecessary.

This book brings together under 'one roof' several topics that I have explored with people who have crossed my life. When invited to, I would share my views and my insights with them based on my personal experience and/or my values and beliefs. It appears that, on many occasions, my insight has been useful, one way or another. Over the years, my observation is that people's challenges revolve around a core group of themes and I explore these in this book.

The book is written in the form of a high level autobiography which covers the aforementioned topics. Each chapter is then followed by a prompt for you to self-scrutinize on that topic. The purpose of each chapter is to initiate a new way of thinking, looking at something in a different light or from a different angle. I talk about my own experiences in each of the topics in the book, not to brag about them, but rather to give an example of a different way to look at things. Everything is based on personal experience and is not made out of theory.

Hence, the book, narrated as my life journey, encourages you to explore the topics that vibrate with you. I encourage you to embrace each challenge as an opportunity for self-growth towards a fulfilled, fun and free life. Life is not complicated if only we simplify it!

Being a woman, my experiences will relate mainly to women, specifically mature women who have gone through some of life's challenges and who are striving to find ways to find serenity, happiness and fulfillment in spite of everything. I say that this can be achieved. It is easy to be a wise and calm person living alone on top of a mountain. True wisdom is when that state can be achieved and maintained whilst living your day to day life with everyone around you having all their demands and imperfections.

If my book motivates one person into a positive change, then it would have completed its purpose. If more than one person is motivated, then the book would have over-achieved its purpose.

Take this journey for you, with me.

* *Some sources of this quote cite Mark Twain, some cite Henry Ford.*

INTRODUCTION

The Beginning

The start of the journey

Today, 26th November 2015, I am 54 years old. I had even forgotten that I was not 54 yet and, when asked how old I was a couple of weeks ago, I said 54. Age has never bothered me really. I think that it is in the mind. I honestly do not feel that I am a different person from the life loving, rebelling mischievous self that I was at 15, 20 and older. Ok, so my body is not as firm as before. I looked at myself naked this morning and smiled and loved my tummy fold that is definitely weighing down towards gravity below. My tummy is the one part of my body that I have never liked. But hey, this is what I have and it is in working order and has performed its job description to the letter as it has stretched three times without complaint providing room for the children that I brought onto this earth. So what do I expect from it!!!! Now with all this stretching and the age, it is drooping down. I love it!

I am extremely happy today and feel on the top of the world. Why would you say do I feel that? Because life is great! Have I achieved the million pounds that once upon a time I wanted to? Nope. Am I travelling the world every six months as I wanted to at one point? No. Do I have the perfect body, the perfect life, the perfect job, the perfect car, the perfect anything? Nope, nope and nope. What I have though is an awareness of wellbeing, of satisfaction and, most of all, of something that is bigger than me and bigger than life. In every challenge that life has gifted me with, I have relentlessly problem-solved and come out the other side bigger, brighter and certainly happier.

It is awesome to have lived on this planet earth for 54 years. I am in a place that many people maybe have never been, or may have been only briefly. This is a place of total happiness, total satisfaction of what I have achieved and what I have not achieved. I am of the old school generation and find this modern life very fast and demanding. So fast indeed that while, very often, I find myself swamped by its waves, I still regain consciousness from time to time and pull myself away from the waves and get to rest and breathe a bit.

Why do I feel that I have to chase that dream and this dream and that other one every day? Why do I feel that I must have all my dreams? I do believe that I can have all my dreams if I apply myself to it. However, I need to know myself enough, understand my situation objectively enough, to filter out what I can chase and have right now and what I have to put on the side for after. The dreams will not burn out but I will. Eventually, things will fall into place by their own accord as long as I apply myself to what I am doing and keep doing something new every time.

I am in a certain hotel this morning and I have just been served a wonderful hot English breakfast in bed. The ultimate birthday present for me! I did not have the luxury to have a lie in because my system decided to wake itself up at 6am. Still, I did not have to rush anywhere and I leisurely got myself ready and decided to put my thoughts on my laptop whilst I waited for the breakfast to arrive. I am in that certain hotel because I am attending a three day book writing course. I have already written a book several years ago that is related to my profession and I did that all by myself and without a book writing course. This time though, I am writing a very serious book with my daughter or, to be exact, my daughter is writing a book with me. I am not sure which one of these two statements is correct. What I mean is that my daughter knows the topic deeply, therefore, is the main writer and I am contributing to it. It is her intellectual property.

Anyway, I am on this book writing boot camp and today is the third and last day of the course and I should really be spending all my spare time contributing to this serious book but, no, not this morning. Today, it is about me and I am writing about me. I am tired of trying too hard, or chasing my tail around, though I do not really have one. I am also tired of doing what everyone else is doing. As a rebel that I am, I am writing this book free style and not following any one of the guidelines that we have been given on this book writing course. My life has been free style and it is fit for me to write free style too. This book is for all who are trying to figure it all out. What is there to figure out anyway?

Many people are surprised by my age when they find out how old I am because they think I look younger than my age. I believe that youthfulness is not just about looks – it is also about attitude, behaviours, mindset and personality. In reply to those people, I have to specify that I did not have my first child in my teens. In fact, I was in my mid-twenties when I had my son. These comments about my age have happened so often that I think that there must be some bit of truth in it. Part of this young phenomena is having my Mum's genes. She passed away in January this year (2015) at the age of 86 and, though she had become very frail and weak with Alzheimer that she had been carrying for many years, she looked fresh and young even on her death bed. The other part of why I look younger is because I act young, I think positive thoughts, I do not worry unnecessarily. I do not let age bother me and I laugh a lot. Most of these things I do naturally without effort. I am naturally a positive person. Being of a mutable sign, for those who know a bit of astrology, I can adapt to circumstances with more flexibility than others. I am also of the fiery Sagitarius birth sign so I erupt quickly and I cool down quickly. Meaning I do not keep grudges, I do not stay in the past and I do not remain in a situation where I am very unhappy for too long. I love fast cars and I do not like to do what others do, or have what others have. I do not stagnate and I am on the move forever looking for improvement. My good friend Tracy recently commented that I am a living dynamo! I am always always chasing something and that is ... drum roll...

1. To know myself better
2. To understand those around me better. I deliberately did not say '<u>know</u> those around me better' because I believe that you never know someone totally. Heck, do I know myself totally, 100 percent? You are joking!!! I am still learning and finding surprises about me. I constantly change each day. What my thoughts were yesterday, they are not today. Today I want pink, tomorrow I want blue... well not literally, I am just making a point.
3. To remain true to myself. To do what I want to do within the confines of my responsibilities to myself and my dependents. I do not try to please everyone, I do not try to do what others are doing and I certainly do not accept an unhappy situation for long.

Ok, so far it has been all about me, me, me and, again, me. Yes it is. My life has been rich in events, in lessons that were learnt and some that were not, in tears, in pain, in laughter, in happiness and in duties. The word 'duty' I do not like! Why do something dutifully? Why not do something because you know it is a duty but you ponder on it and 'choose' to do it as opposed to blindly following it through because it is your duty.

I am someone who chooses to do things with awareness and, when I do something, I (usually) do not expect anything in return. I have realised that many of my disappointments have been because I would expect something from someone or I would want someone to behave in a certain manner or say something I want to hear. How selfish is that? What right do I have to expect something from someone who does not have it in the first place to give? Can I expect a pineapple to give me apple juice - in its natural form I mean? Can I expect a cow to give birth to a human baby? Who knows, maybe in a crazy future (the far away future I hope when I have departed this earth) we will be able to do those insane things. The way that science is moving so fast nowadays... I am just making a point here.

This book is about dropping the act. Let me drop my act and bare it all in this book. I am dumping (literally) my thoughts on paper and I am not going through following the steps of writing a 'good' book. Hey, I will do that when doing my serious book but, for this one, I am going to have fun. You may not have fun reading some of the things I will say in this book because you do not agree with them and that is totally alright. I am only responsible for myself and not for anyone else. So if you do not agree with me, then you are fine and I am fine too.

As I am writing my thoughts down, I don't even know what my chapters will be about. All I know is that I have many things to talk about. I will keep it evolved around the topic of positively problem solving when conventional ways do not work, and keeping lasting results from those decisions.

So let's get some form of structure to this book. I am going to be writing about me. I will be asking myself questions and answering them. I will be sharing my experiences, real experiences, nothing fake in here though I won't give you too much detail or I might bore you. Who wants to hear about someone else's story for too long? You may find similarities or messages in what you read. Something might resonate with you. Developmental books are usually written to you or to people generally. For example, I just opened a motivational book and I quote 'If we are not vigilant, being around constant worry can quickly limit who we are and what we might be capable of.' Here is another example from a leadership book and I quote 'Even when you're alive with a future you want and you've engaged people there will still be forces working against you delivering brilliantly through others.' I want to be different. I won't be talking to you or at you and I will be talking mainly about me. In doing so, I am not assuming that you need help in any of the topics that I am covering. If anything that I say resounds with you and gives you an insight or a thought that you have not explored before, then the aim of my book has been fulfilled. Everything that I cover in this book is based on personal experience. This is not a book where I theorise or philosophise based on something I have read or come across. Let's begin.

You can use the topics in this book as a sounding board based on the experiences that I am sharing with you. After each topic, there is a free-style notes section which you can use as a workbook for you to write down your own notes, goals and outcomes and action points. I write a few prompts in that section only to guide you along. You might choose to ignore those prompts completely and make your own notes. You may even write some notes about something you want to contact me about relating to the topic. It is your book so you use it however you wish to. Hey you can even write your shopping list here. It is your book, and you write whatever you wish in there. In fact, you might even want to start writing a book yourself and I would love to read it. In fact, how about I create a space on a website online and you write about yourself or you share what is similar between you and I and you can create it as a little ebook. This is an idea that has just spouted out as I was writing this section. It might be a crazy idea – I prefer to call it a freestyle idea. How about maybe you pass on a message to your children, your parents, your husband or the public in general by putting some topics about you in a little ebook. Blogging is common.... Let's take it a step further and make mini ebooks of ourselves. Even more crazier, I may even be willing to go on Facebook just to allow more people to share their views and comments about people creating and sharing ebooks of themselves. Being on Facebook would be a huge deal for me because, so far, I have not been attracted to having virtual relationships with anyone.

I am not even printing lines on the free-style pages so it remains free style. How can I assume that everyone writes on lines of a certain length and certain space in between. It is blank – write how you wish – from bottom to top, from right to left, from the middle out.... Do something totally different as you see fit.

Introduction/The Beginning Free-style Notes

- What is your beginning?
- Where did you start your journey?
- How has your past shaped you?
- How would you have preferred your past to shape you, and what can you do about it?

Identity

Who I am

Who I was then...

I very often got confused about who I was and I wandered around like a lost person thinking I am the mother, the sister, the wife, the employee.... you name it... that I perform each day.

I was born and brought up in a lovely island in the Indian Ocean – Mauritius. I am the youngest of five children and I have been loved and spoilt by my father, mother, sisters and brothers. Being the youngest one, I guess I got away with many things. Plus I was quite cute... so.... you figure it out. I grew up being very confident within myself and, from an early age, I was quite strong minded.

My father used to drink alcohol quite often. He was domineering and violent towards my mother and had mistresses. My Mum, in my view, was a weak woman who allowed her husband to abuse her in such ways. Well, that was my view of the situation. So, at a very young age, I formulated the opinion that I would never ever let a man:

1. Be unfaithful to me
2. Be violent towards me

I carried this belief into my adult life and, to this day, I adhere closely to this rule. Another by-product of my dad's behaviour is that I do not tolerate drunk people around me. Though I was empathic towards my mum being in such a relationship with my father, I, nevertheless associated myself with my father more than my mum in relation to strength of character and drive. Over the years, I observed that my father and my mother were the wrong match for each other. My father, being an extremely cultured, educated and charmingly extroverted person would (maybe) have thrived with a woman that could handle his personality. Someone who could encourage and support him and, indeed, walk side by side with him. Instead, my mother was a timid, introverted, primary school educated and very religious person who would put her children before herself and her husband at any time. I do not agree with that concept. Sometimes I need to put my children first, especially when they are quite young and dependent on me. Sometimes I need to put 'me' first (that is a must to keep my sanity), and sometimes I need to put my husband first (totally a must too). How would a mother juggle to fulfill all these aspects and demands on her? Well go figure, but somehow one needs to be able to do this. I never did get the balance right....

I left Mauritius at the age of 23 and travelled to England to get married. I ended up marrying the brother of the man I was supposed to marry (it is a long story for another book), had two children and then left him after six years of marriage when he started getting jealous and became physically violent. I say 'started' to become violent because the second time that he lifted his hands on me, I was gone with the children in the middle of the night and with only our clothes on our back. I did not even have a purse, a handbag, a toothbrush. There was a short moment of opportunity to leave the house and I did not think of anything else. My two children were just about nearly four and two. From the police station where we ran to for safety, we ended up in a refuge and I have never looked back. That was the first implementation of the lessons I had learnt as a child with regards to my parents' relationship. I would not have stayed long enough for my husband to beat me hard enough to get me into hospital. My Mum used to say 'once a man has raised his hand over a woman, he will never stop'. It is amazing the things that stick in your mind. I have come across women who had been beaten black and blue by a man, one even had broken ribs and had to be hospitalised and, yet, the woman would still end up back with the man. I could not understand it at the time and I still cannot but I appreciate that we are all on our individual paths and we all have different situations and personalities.

Leaving my husband then was the best thing that I could have ever done, both for myself and for my two children. I owed it to myself, and I owed it to them to ensure that we would live in a harmonious home where a father is not beating up the mother and where they would not be witnessing arguments all the time. That is something that no child should ever have to witness like I, and my siblings, had witnessed when we were growing up. My children did witness arguments and that would be mainly my arguments with one of them or all of them but they have not witnessed me arguing with a husband or a partner.

For many years, I literally rebuilt my life and a home for my two children. We were first put in a bed and breakfast and then re-housed in a council flat. I went to university to do a four year degree course and became a full time student on top of being mum and dad for my children. It was tough but I had peace of mind and my world consisted of the children and me.

Who was I then???? Pretty much 'mummy' and nothing else. The children were so young that even the student part of my life was insignificant. I then met a handsome and very pleasant young man while I was at university. He is the man who actually took the rosebud that I was and turned it into a flourishing young rose. In French it is 'épanouir un bouton de rose'. This description is always what comes to my mind when I think about the role he played in my life. So after I met him, the 'who I am' split into becoming a lover as well. So here I was being a mother, a student and a lover. Our relationship was deep and passionate, the type of passion where it is either extremely high or extremely low. No in-between. When we were good, we were gooooooood, when we were not good, we were reaaaalllly not good. Well he is a fire sign and I am a fire sign so what do you expect?? We had a very long relationship, on and off, for about 18 years. Out of that wonderful relationship, my third and youngest child was born. So now I was Mum to two older children and a young baby.

This 18 year old relationship was key into molding me into who I am today, and provided me invaluable lessons that have served me well but were extremely painful at the time. I would say that my mum and my father were my first life teachers, and my 18 year relationship was my second life churning teaching experience. My most significant teaching has been through raising my three children. To be specific, my eldest daughter, Rebekha, my middle child has been the most challenging and most rewarding of all. Because of her, I would not want to come back to my home and wished I could just go somewhere else after work. For her, I enrolled and studied astrology for a year. This has served me extremely well in understanding some characteristics about her being and personality. All my three children are from the birth sign of Taurus and they are earthy people. So by studying astrology I learnt a lot about all of them at once. Ironically, that same middle child, my eldest daughter, Rebekha, has now become one of the closest (if not the closest) people that know me very well and, in many ways, she uncannily has adapted many traits from me. In fact, we are now doing a business together, so not only do we have to put up with each other as mother and daughter but also as business partners.

After I finished my four year degree, as well as being a mum and a lover, I swapped my student role and became an employee and started building my career. So here I am now and the 'who I am' is

- Mother as a predominant role because I do not have a break from being a mother when I have young or dependent children.
- Employee and career builder as another predominant role because I need to improve my skills and gain experience to be able to reach my professional and financial goals.

- Lover because I need a personal life and have my own needs met, that keep things in balance even though having a love life does bring a lot of additional drama.... But also brings some amazingly extraordinary fulfillment.

This is who I was for several years until the children grew older...

Who I am now

Many years on, I am totally fulfilled as a mother as my children are all very close to me and I am even a grandmother. I have a fulfilling career and have built a strong reputation in my specialism. My 18 year relationship ended followed by my next significant relationship with the man who I can only describe as my 'oasis' and my grounding force. His earthy nature positively tames my fiery composition. We have now been in a relationship for eight years and got married two years ago.

So who am I now? I do not have any dependents anymore. My youngest is now at university since September and, for the first time in my whole 54 years' life span, I live without a child in the house. It feels amazing and fabulous to not be a full time mum anymore.

Now I feel that I am everything and nothing. I am an actor acting the theatre of life and I perform multiple roles as it seems fit and as I feel like. I do not have young dependent children anymore so I can choose not to be a mother. I am a wife and I can choose to be a wife sometimes, I am a grandmother and my daughter 'forces' me to be a grandmother many times but I choose to accept to be forced into that or not. I am also a friend, a coach, a mentor, a sister, a student (because I never ever stop studying and learning new things about myself) and so on and so on. When I am not all these roles, I am just me, someone that likes her own company. A woman who loves the sound of nothingness and who loves looking within and finding out who and what rattles her during the times that something manages to rattle her. I am at that age where I do not have to pretend, where I do not have to be anybody else but myself, where my children know me enough and I know them enough to be able to give each other the space that we need from each other; and to crowd each other when we choose and want to. When I take on a role, I take it deliberately and knowingly. Before, the role would take me over. Not anymore.

I know myself enough to be aware of the characteristics that I was born with, and to improve the ones that serve me. For those that do not serve me, I drop them or I mould them into serving me. I know my limitations as a woman, and so I work within those parameters because I know them. The fact that I can be short tempered is not who I am. The fact that I can be harsh and say it as it is is not who I am. The fact that I forget names easily is not who I am either. I find my happiness within; my reference is always within. Yes, life throws pain and challenges at me when needed. I then hurt, I cry if I need to cry, I feel sorry for myself long enough to make myself feel better and then I always look within and find out more things about 'me'. I always say to my children – 'it is all about you, always, and never about anyone else'.

Who I am is that space deep within myself that I cannot find sometimes, because I am so busy letting myself get carried away by what I think I want instead of letting myself be inspired by what I need. What I need is learn to know who I am and who I want to be in all aspects of my life and in all the roles that I play. Who I am is letting go and allowing in. I am not the body; the body will die and rot. What will remain is all the work that I have done on that awareness that I call myself to turn a trait that I was born with (not a physical trait but the type of trait that you cannot touch) into an even more beautiful and fulfilling trait that is not just beautiful to me but to all the people that I touch.

I am nothing as in nothingness and not in the sense of inferiority or belittle. When I am nothing, I can be anyone or anything I want to be. When I am busy being somebody, I am limiting what else I can be because there are only so many roles that I can juggle at any one time. So when I strip myself to nothingness, I allow myself the option to rebuild myself as someone else that is devoid of those attributes that I do not need or want any more in my life. I allow myself to also strip out of my immediate circle those that I do not need or want any more in my life. I am the legendary phoenix that I can build and rebuild from the ashes day after day into who I want.

Who I am is bigger than the words I can use to describe it. When you strip all the roles I have mentioned above – and there are even some that I have not mentioned – there is a bigger 'I' (if I may call it this) that is left, an 'I' that is bigger than the sum of all the above. This is who I truly am.

Identity Free-style Notes

- Who are you?
- Do you like 'you'?
- Who do you want to be?
- What can you do to become that person/that being?

Boundaries

Space Clarity

I am someone who does not like things to be fuzzy in my relationships with people. I like to know exactly where I stand and I like to let others know where they stand too. For example, when I meet a man and he is interested in me in terms of having a relationship, I usually say two things – 'I like to flirt' and 'I demand a lot from a man'. The usual response I get is a giggle and a brushing aside of my statements. Maybe my words are seen as part of the 'courting' game, whatever that game is. However, I am always very serious. These are two things that any man who is interested in me should know.

Likewise, with my children, I let them know what I will put up with and what I will not. I do not like children lying for no reason and there are certain rules that, if broken, will result in catastrophic consequences. I think that all of my children have broken at least one of my sacred rules and they have felt the consequences. My eldest daughter, Rebekha, has been the most rebellious and challenging and she has experienced my worst consequences which incidentally have served her to become a fine and independent adult. Yet, as mentioned earlier, we have both evolved now and she is the person that understands me the most and bears many of my traits – the good ones and the not so good ones too. Now, as adults, the children joke about my 'once upon a time' disciplinary style and we have a good laugh about it.

Professionally, I am clear of what my role involves and I take pride in developing myself through courses, research and self-development materials to become the best at what I do. To me, work is not just about money, a big part of it is about enjoying what I do and working with people that have integrity. The corporate world can be full of politics and big egos. I know my strengths professionally as well as my weaknesses. When I am not happy about something, I say it but I keep it to the professionalism that is required and I always keep progressing whatever I am working on regardless. I do not take things personally, actually let me rephrase this, when I take it personally, I go away and work on myself and turn the situation into an objective professional situation. I do not mix my personal life with my professional life and, at work, I am the utmost professional person that I can be.

In my personal relationship (i.e. with my man) he will know what I will put up with and what I will not. I will accept a lot of things from someone but once I have reached my limit, there is no turning back. The way I see it, I want to go forward, I do not want to stagnate, I do not want to stay in the past and the present is the only time we have. Of course, I think and plan for the future to a certain extent. How do I know whether I will be there tomorrow? So the best time is now.

These are examples of how knowing and keeping to my boundaries helps me avoid getting into sticky situations. I say avoid because one thing that some people think they can do is change me or I think that I can change them. When I catch myself trying to change someone, I pull myself back, look at myself from within and find my center again and start over. Really, who am I to be wanting to change someone, and besides it is extra work that I do not need. So, I do my best not to start the crusade of changing people.

There may be many things that I don't like with those very close to me. However, they are things that are not such priorities otherwise they would not be close to me. I am sure there are many things about me that people do not like either. With children it is different because whether you want to or not you end up having to love them regardless. Just like me though, everyone around me changes. As my good friend Katie, in North Carolina, always says 'Nothing is constant but change itself'. So my boundaries change as well. The way I was strict with my older two children changed with my youngest one. Firstly my personal situation was different, I was established in my career when I had my youngest whereas I was juggling university with raising two young children with my older ones. I was, therefore, more financially secure and more mature too. I had learnt a lot of lessons from raising the older two children. The way I dealt with challenges with my children was different. Losing my temper with my older children was never something that I enjoyed. I used to lose my temper at the drop of a pin and I am glad to say that I have now developed more tolerance and patience. So my younger daughter benefitted from that 'maturity' (if you can call it that), and I guess I mellowed out as I got older.

My two oldest children, Reuben and Rebekha, never skip an opportunity to remind Jasmine, my youngest, how she had it easy and did not have my frequent and fierce 'eruptions' to deal with. They tell me I have become soft in my older age.

Boundaries Free-style Notes

- Do you have boundaries?
- Do people know about your boundaries – you may have different ones for different people? In fact, are you even aware of what your boundaries are? Sometimes, you may be frustrated with people and it could be related to boundaries.
- Be clear on the things that you choose to tolerate and those that you will not compromise on at any cost. That way, if faced with a cross over on your boundary, your brain is geared towards the correct line of action that will serve you best.

Expectations

My Expectations of Others

Ah! This is a biggie. I have mentioned it briefly before. I find the whole thing about expectation fascinating. Don't get me wrong, I expect from others as well... when I am in my non-awareness zone, my blind spot zone. I hear people around me saying things like "I have to do this", "I must do that" with regards a relationship with someone else. I have the same thoughts and then I ask myself "why do I <u>have to</u>?"; "have to" is another word that sits in the same bucket as "it is my duty to". I get a physiological reaction to these words. So I would ask myself "why do I have to?" and then answer the question. Only then would I <u>choose </u>to do the thing or not. For me, just this process changes the whole perspective and I feel in control of doing that thing whatever it may be, instead of 'having' to do it.

So today, on my birthday, my eldest daughter, Rebekha, (as expected!) sent me an email with a very funny ecard and lots of loving words to wish me Happy Birthday. She is someone who always remembers and finds a way of making someone's birthday very special. I will tell you something that she did for one of her birthdays in a moment. So, she wishes me happy birthday. My youngest daughter, Jasmine, calls me in the morning and again around lunchtime from her university to say hello as she usually does. On her second call she says "I hope you are having a good day Mummy" and I replied "I am. It is my birthday today". There is a short silence and a shuffle and words of profuse apologies start coming out of her mouth; I cut her short saying "If you wish me happy birthday now it would be great" and she did. My daughter being who she is, I would not be surprised that she would have been bothered all day about having forgotten about my birthday. I found it very funny and I totally enjoyed putting her on the spot and getting my birthday wishes. My son, totally forgot too. It is brilliant! Why should I expect them all to remember my birthday? They have their life to live. My youngest daughter has been busy applying for a university exchange with a tight deadline. My son is busy working every day. Do they love me less because they did not remember to wish me happy birthday? That's crazy.

When I do something for someone, I do not expect things in return. Of course, when the children were younger, I would expect them to tidy their bedroom, to do their homework, to do the dishes and to behave themselves. This is not what I am talking about. I am talking about my expectations from other adults including my children who are now adults too. I find myself exhilaratingly happy not to have to think for my children and make decisions for them. I am free now to be myself!!!!!

Christmas is coming up and this is another expectation that I do not put on my shoulders. If my children come to spend Christmas with me fine, if they prefer to go somewhere else fine.

More and more I am learning to let go of things, including expectations. It is not because I have a low opinion of someone that I do not have an expectation of someone and do not believe the person will deliver. It is just that I am leaving the space free for one thing or another to fill it up.

Here is the thing I told you that I would share with you regarding Rebekha. One day a few years ago, she turned up at my doorstep on her birthday with a big bouquet of flowers. When I opened the door, she handed me the bouquet and thanked me for having gone through labor pains for her and given her a birthday to celebrate. So her idea of celebrating that particular birthday was to celebrate the woman who gave birth to her. Of course, my eyes welled up with tears. It was totally unexpected and the emotional feeling was amazing.

14

On several occasions, I have experienced receiving what I wanted to get in the first place once I let go of that thing. For example I would be trying so hard to meet up with my man, planning here, planning there and I am getting frustrated that this is not happening for whatever reason. Then I would just let it go – not out of defeat but as me trusting that it will happen when it needs to happen – and then magically life will conspire to make it happen effortlessly and unexpectedly. When I receive something unexpectedly, the pleasure intensifies even more.

I used to have expectations on what I should be doing on a Saturday or a Sunday. I would plan this and that and would know exactly what I would have completed at the end of that day. As the day evolved, there would be a delay here (maybe traffic or I had a bad sleep and started the day later than planned), then another thing going on there.... and my level of frustration would rise and rise ending into a bad day and totally upset about not having done what I wanted to do. Nowadays, we know better. I say 'we' because my daughters, especially Rebekha, have witnessed how a planned day can just take its own turn and end up totally the opposite of what was planned. What we have observed is that if we plan the day loosely and then let it unfold, things that we would not have thought of doing would happen – sometimes quite enjoyable and magical things. When we do this, we end up with a few perks:

- We remain relaxed and, as a game, let the day do its thing
- We practice our planning skills because sometimes we have to re-work the plan to fit the day
- We get to do the things that we need to do instead of the things that we 'wanted' to do and every time, without fail, it turns out better in the long run. Yes, we do not get to complete whatever we had planned that day but, hey, life does not stop there

Letting go is a freeing feeling. Totally amazing. It takes responsibility out of my hands. I am not talking about my responsibility to myself and my dependents (if I have any) here. I am still responsible to start the day and when things start taking a different route, I adapt to that new journey. Another way of explaining this is to say that I become flexible to the day and to life.

My Expectations of Self

Expectation is not always directed to or coming from the external world. Sometimes I have an expectation from myself and I end up beating myself up and/or feeling guilty in some way. I was brought up in a way that the house had to be clean and tidy all the time. That was ok when I was living in my parents' house and I was studying or working. I had the time to do my share of the chores. I brought that habit with me in England. I used to clean and tidy up and every time there would be more to do. Then I became a university student with two young children and no husband to share the chores with me. The expectation that I had from myself to keep the house clean and tidy all the time soon disappeared. I like a clean house, no doubt about that. When I am extremely tired though I would favour my sleep over dishes that need to be washed. I have realised that tidying up and cleaning never ends whereas my ability to function at a maximum level has a quick end when I am tired. I am a dragon, a real monster, when I am tired and everyone needs to stay out of my way. Now I relax. There are certain things that need to be clean always, like the toilet and the wash-basin and my bedroom – I need to have at least one neat area where I can chill – but otherwise things can wait until the next day.

I also used to always agree to any party or event I was invited to. Then typically, as the day approaches, I would not feel like going anymore, either due to being tired or some other reason. I would force myself to still go and would wait until a decent amount of time had passed before I would make my exit without seeming too rude. My friends would always comment on how I am always leaving get togethers early. Well I need at least eight hours sleep to function properly and I am an early bird, so no surprise that I want to be home by 9pm.

Nowadays, I do not expect myself to do something that I really do not want to. I would call and tell the person that I am not coming even if I had agreed to it already. And... I would not beat myself about not putting others before me all the time. I have put the children first for so many years, now it is time that I put 'me' first.

Others' Expectations of Me

Hah! This is an interesting one. I used to follow what was expected of me blindly – what my parents expect (actually, this is a bit of a lie as I was quite a rebellious child when I was growing up), what my friends expect, what my neighbours expect, what my relatives expect... the list goes on. Now, I start by evaluating what I need to adhere to and what I do not need to. I treat my profession differently though. I am paid to deliver something in my work, so that is exactly what I do even if I am not too happy about it. While fulfilling my side of the bargain, I will be finding ways to get out of the situation and I never stay in an unpleasant situation for long. My answer to those who keep moaning about a situation and do not do anything about it is to do something to change it or keep quiet and get on with it. I have encouraged many of my friends and colleagues to make changes to areas of their life/profession that they can influence. I am happy and willing to help anyone who is willing to help himself/herself.

Expectations Free-style Notes

- What are the expectations that bring you the most frustrations regularly?
- How does frustration serve you today?
- If it is not, change your expectation or the expectation that others have on you.
- What expectations do you burden yourself with and you end up beating yourself about?
- What expectations do you press on others that do not serve them and do not serve you?

Goal Settings

Aim, Shoot, Goal!

Before I even knew about goals, I had goals. For me a goal is making a step forward, however small or big.

When I just got married for the first time, I was totally dependent on my husband. I was extremely homesick and having been used to a closely knit family in my homeland, I was suddenly in this strange country where people did not kiss, hug or shake hands. This was the biggest challenge for me when I came to England. My husband had a lot of good attributes and showing affection was not one of his best. I actually physically missed human touch. In Mauritius, when women greet each other, we kiss on the cheek. Children would kiss their parents when going out or coming back in the house even when still living together. Men would greet each other by shaking hands. Women would greet men that they do not know well by shaking hands otherwise it would be a kiss on the cheek too. That is a lot of touch that I would get in my day to day life. Girls at schools and colleges would walk hand in hand innocently just to show closeness and loving friendship to each other. We would touch each other when talking, nothing dodgy here, just like touching a forearm or a shoulder – put it down to being an exotic island and so we would talk with our hands. To be cut off suddenly from such a warm and 'touchy' culture was the hardest.

I am really pleased now to see that the English culture has absorbed other influences and people have become more warm and touchy. I hug my friends and close colleagues, male and females. Even kissing – wait for this – on both cheeks has become the norm. Amazing, fantastically amazing! This is great progress!

I digressed again… so I was saying that I was totally dependent on my husband – financially, emotionally, physically, you name it. He had the role of my husband, my father, my mother, my siblings, everything. Remember that in those days, we did not have a mobile phone, we did not have Skype, we did not even have a phone in the house. It was tough. Me, naturally being an independent person, I decided that I needed to start working and earning some money. So I became a nanny looking after a baby. Then I joined one of those temporary agencies and I was sent to a factory – I think it was a sausage factory. I went there for only one day. Then my husband and I went to stay in a private compound where four families were living and the woman from each family unit had a physical impairment. So my husband (at the time) and I, as well as another couple, lived on site to provide various practical services to those families.

After my two children were born, I started realising that while my husband had very good intentions to provide for me and the children, his mindset was not geared towards doing this systematically. I decided to go to work and this is when I started becoming more and more independent. I started working as a temporary psychiatric PA (Personal Assistant) and I enjoyed what I was doing. It was very interesting to read about the cases that the psychiatrists were dealing with as I typed up their notes. One of them was a forensic psychiatrist. Wow! It opened my eyes to the circumstances that some people live in out there in the world. My life had been so sheltered!

Then one day, when I was typing up some hand written letters as part of my job, I thought 'I can do better than that'. The letters that I used to type for one particular person, who had all these diplomas and was in a high place professionally, were full of mistakes – grammar, spelling, etc. That is when I decided that I would go to university, get a degree and have a career that would be financially more rewarding than being a PA (Personal Assistant). At that stage, my husband was having difficulty dealing with my growing independence from him and this is when he started showing signs of jealousy which resulted in the story above where I took my two children, left him and never turned back.

I attended university full time for four years. After obtaining my degree, I decided that I did not want to live in a council flat for ever and so I bought a house. I moved in the house a week after my youngest was born in April 1996.

Then followed a long journey of self-development and searching for 'me'. Life had provided me with a secure shelter in the form of my home and it was ready to bash me around for the next stage of my personal teachings. The challenges were many and deep in the form of my partner at the time and my children. Professionally, I was good and did not (thankfully) go through any painful challenges on that front. In terms of friendship, no challenges there. With regards to my parents and siblings, no challenges there either. I felt love, understanding and support in these areas at all time. My teachings were focused on those closest to me – my partner and children.

I decided to study astrology to understand my children better and attended an evening course for a year. It was an eye opener with regards to my children. As mentioned earlier, they are all from the birth sign of Taurus of the element of Earth. They have been my greatest teacher – actually, that is not totally correct – my eldest daughter, Rebekha, has been my greatest teacher. When it came to life teaching, she would get the award of the Grand Master. Don't be mistaken, I had my fair share of challenges with Reuben too; however, Rebekha... wow...she pushed me to another zone altogether.

Professionally, I had attended courses, self-development seminars, created a mentor programme and even written and self-published a book about my profession which still to this day provides me with some royalties. People are still buying this book even though some contents would be out dated now. Maybe my next book should be to relaunch an updated version of that book.

Goal setting for me is a given, a "taken for granted" each day that I live. They are part of an intuitive process. There are the bigger ones like buying a house and there are some little (but huge ones) such as making something better about myself today, like not judging someone or listening to someone or making time for someone. These are all goals that are as important in making me who I am.

I would say that my whole life has been goal driven. I remember in my pre-teens days, I wanted to be a nun, then it was an air hostess then it was a yogi – they are all goals right? Ok, those were maybe unrealistic but it was something that I aspired to for a very brief time span. I change some of my goals, some others I do not complete and it is all ok. I change every day so why would my goals remain static. Today I want blue, tomorrow I want yellow – so what? If someone says "you have changed your mind" I would simply say "yes".

Even on the day that I am dying, I will have a goal such as taking my last breath with peace and serenity and having a wide smile on my face. I can't imagine how exciting it would be to finally find out what lies behind that ultimate final curtain!!!

Some people have asked me, how do I keep going? How do I find the energy? My answer is – "how not to"?

Goal Setting Free-style Notes

- What are your current goals?
- Why do you have these goals?
- What step(s) are you taking to reach the most urgent one? Is it working? Do you need to adjust your track to reaching your goal?

Religion and Spirituality

The seen and unseen

Oooohh... taboo... I am on shaky grounds here and treading a thin line.... Hey this is about me so what I write does not invalidate what you think on this topic. So let me start treading.... This section is dedicated specifically to my good friend Terry. I would have lost his interest from the start of the title of this section. Terry, here is to your spirituality!

I was born and raised in a practising Roman Catholic family and this served me very well while I was growing up. Even at a young age, though, I would take what felt right to me from religion and I would leave what did not. For example, I would not pray to all the various male and female saints and would prefer to pray direct to God. I did not even pray to Jesus really. The Virgin Mary, however, yes I saw her as a Mother figure and I would pray to her. My view was why go through the messengers if you have access to the Boss.

Nowadays, I talk to a Bigger Entity/Energy/Being... whatever word you wish to use; a Force that does not have the sad traits that, as a human, I have. A Force that is constant and loving even if I have 'sinned' and is not bribed by treating me better than others if I promise to do this or that. I talk and I do not pray. I argue and I do not pray. My view of praying is that I am negotiating something where I would end up the winner – i.e. I would get something I want and maybe in return I would promise to do something if I get that thing. If I have a prayer it is about me being able to change myself and not about my circumstance or situation changing. Remember I always make everything about me so spirituality is about me too.

The way I see it, religion is man-made and spirituality is self-made. Each has its purpose and its phase. For me, religion served me wonderfully well from my childhood until I was in my late twenties. Then I started searching for more. My experience of religion is that very often it is one rule in the church on Sunday and another rule when I am outside the church. People would be friendly and even touch hands during the Sharing of Graces and then on leaving the church would look straight ahead and forget about the brotherhood in God. Someone would have just shaken my hand in peace during the church ceremony and then see me struggle with my bags or children after leaving the church and look right ahead. Am I religious? No. Am I spiritual? Yes. I brought up my children by choice to follow the practice of the religion I was brought up in. Why? Because this framework really helped me when I was growing up. So I allowed them that same framework knowing that it would come a time when they would be asking their own questions and searching for their own path.

Religion in England and Mauritius is very different. In my homeland, going to Sunday mass and participating in religious rituals and festivities is fun, it is something that young people do and enjoy doing. That is how it was in the days that I was living there. In England, Sunday mass is still very traditional with traditional songs. Therefore, it was not long before my children, as soon as each of them reached a certain age, started dismissing religion and finding their own way.

My spirituality is in my heart. It is what I do at each moment, what I think at each moment and what I say at each moment. It is about me improving the traits and attributes that I was born with. When I lack patience, I build more patience. When I am irritable, I build my tolerance. When I start judging, I look at myself and reconnect – well at least I try. Sometimes I succeed and sometimes not; regardless I start again and soon it will become a habit.

I respect others' beliefs and views. When I am conversing with someone and I do not agree with what is being said about religion or spirituality, I don't say anything. I might choose to share my thoughts with the person or I might decide to be quiet. Each of us has individual experiences and those experiences leave a mark in a different way. Even if we are both from the same family, from the same parents, from the same environment, having had the same teachings growing up, our impressions of the world may be quite wide apart. My siblings and I each have a different take on religion and spirituality. I used to have a compelling need to get people to agree with my views and it would, most times than not, leave me tired of having had to debate my case. Now, I just relax, sit back and observe the situation, usually with a smile on my face. I really enjoy doing this especially when I am in a group. It is fascinating to watch how much effort people put into trying to convince each other of their point of view. From time to time, my passionate self would take over and I would get pulled into the debate and start defending my position. Hah! It is so funny when I do that. Then I laugh at myself afterwards. Who am I trying to convince? The others or just myself? When I let go it is just amazing and so much less tiring.

Spirituality is something that I work on daily by reading the materials that resonate with me, by watching what elevates me, by being with those that motivate me. In that sense, I jealously guard myself against what comes through my senses. I know there are 'bad' things that happen every day in the world. I do not need to read or listen to the details for re-affirmation. I prefer to use my thoughts to project rippling and positive waves to the world. It is said that we are connected to one another via an energy field. So my thoughts would impact that energy field – positive and negative. What others do, they do. What I do matters to me so I choose to think positive thoughts, say empowering and motivating words and do loving and caring actions. Can you imagine if each person was to be totally responsible for each word that came out of his mouth, how much pain could be avoided? Words can hurt as much as a blow can. For a person to be responsible for his word, he would have to monitor his thought and then the word would follow. So double whammy, thoughts and words would be more positive and loving and in synergy. What an effect on our energy field!

Religion and Spirituality Free-style Notes

- What is your religion and why?
- Does it serve you well?
- What gives you balance and purpose?

True Love

Unconditional... really?

This is one of my favourite topics – True Love, Unconditional Love. When the tough gets going, that is when I know about the authenticity of that love...

My take on true love is when I love someone enough to set him free for his happiness, not mine. What I mean is that I am willing to go against my wishes and desires for the pleasure of that person. When I say 'love someone' I am referring to any type of love – between a couple, a parent and child, between friends and so on. As an example, my boyfriend is not happy with me anymore and he has found someone that he is really happy with. After going through whatever emotions and insecurities that this brings out in me, do I love him enough to genuinely want his happiness? So much that I would rather he was with another woman happy rather than with me unhappy! Do I love my child enough to do things for him and not expect anything – I mean anything – in return? When he introduces me to the woman of his dreams, do I love him enough to truly, really truly, give him my blessing genuinely and embrace that woman in the family even though I hate the sight of her or I see her as the other woman who is taking my son's attention and love from me? We know the tie that is between sons and mothers. It amazes me how many mothers cannot let go of their sons fully. I have had personal experience with this and so I have promised myself to never be that type of mother to my son. I cannot speak about the tie that exists between fathers and daughters as I have not experienced being a father. Being a mother to a son is such a huge responsibility, in my view.

How he will treat a woman in the future, how respectful he will be of his woman, how supportive he will be, all this may be influenced with his experience of his relationship with me, his mother. I find this responsibility huge! Thankfully, my son is an adult now and, from what I have seen so far, I have not done a bad job. So many men – grown up men – still allow their mother to influence them and interfere in their personal life. Shocking!!! I am not talking about when a son looks after his Mum as a child would look after a parent due to love and respect. I am talking about mothers who interfere, who demand, who make judgments and are just in their son's business.

True love is loving enough to let go. There is the notion of unconditional love! Just the word 'unconditional' does not convey something positive for me. As a mother, I do not have a choice but love my children. Sometimes I do not like them, many times they do not like me either. Nothing we can do about this, we are stuck with each other; if not physically but with the ties of parent and child. However, on the whole they love me and I love them. They can only have one mother and I brought these children onto this earth. Nature almost dictates that I love them against my own free will. In fact, there is no free will here, it is an instinct that is within my cells. Is that unconditional love? No, that is Nature's love.

True love is when I can rise above myself to still love someone who has wronged me. It is very easy to love someone who makes me feel good, who gives me presents and who tells me pleasant things. When it is not so, is it as easy? True love is not about letting myself being walked over, or being taken advantage of. It is about genuinely forgiving and forgetting and allowing the person to start over without expecting the person to fault again as before. It is about giving freely and receiving freely. I need to be able to truly love and forgive myself too before I can practice this on someone else.

True love is not about proximity. I can be physically close to someone yet be as far apart from each other as the North and

South poles. In contrast, I could be miles away from someone and be as close to him as a glove on my hand. I have experienced this and it is wonderfully amazing. True love is wanting the other person to succeed because his success is my success. True love is wanting the other person to be happy because his happiness is my happiness. When the other person also shares a true love with me, my desires and wishes become his desires and wishes. Then I do not have to worry about them anymore because he is fulfilling them and vice versa. This can be a complex concept to grasp and yet it can be so simple.

My personal experience of unconditional love is that there is some form of expectation at the end and, as mentioned above, expectation breeds frustrations.

Have I experienced giving true love? I try every time I have the opportunity. I have had glimpses of how it feels and it is magical. It is freedom.

True Love Free-style Notes

- What is your take on true love?
- Do you practice it in your life and who with?
- Do you get it from others? If not, why not?

Stand Out

Know the Rules

I cannot understand why a lot of people want to be like someone else. From an early age, I wanted to be different. This has followed me into my adult years. If everyone wants this brand of car, I want a different car. If the trend is seaside holidays, I want to have my holiday in the forest. It is most likely my ego, not wanting to be labeled like everyone else. I like it because it serves me well on many occasions.

Our friends, our loved ones, all those who mean well want us to be the person they are used to, comfortable with and that fit within their comfort zones. This is a generalisation I am making because now I do not have this problem as I am very careful who I allow to be close to me. On various self-development seminars, I often hear people say that their loved ones do not know that they are attending this and that course. Sometimes it is even a partner or husband because he/she would not understand and would be disparaging. Who wants to hear words that discourages or puts us down? I often say to my children "if you do not have something nice to say, do not say anything". All three of them have a habit of calling each other insulting names jokingly when they get together usually at my place. This is a behaviour that I have never endorsed and I am always telling these big children adults of mine off. I have been brought up in a family where I had never heard a swear word. The first time I heard my older brother swear, we were in a taxi on our way to a wedding and I was about 15 or 16. He was not even swearing as in swearing at someone, he swore as part of his conversation with the taxi driver. It was not even like a hard swearing but I was shocked hearing it coming from my brother!

Has my upbringing contributed in me being different from others? I guess so. Nowadays, it is a conscious decision to be similar to others when I need to and to be different when I want to. There is a place and a time for everything. At work, I get on with my work and I conform where I need to. For many years I have worked in the City of London in prestigious corporate organisations and I know what my image and behaviour should be when I am conducting meetings, making presentations or managing people. Is this the place to be drastically different? No – unless I don't want to be taken seriously.

I have a motto – never ever do or say something that will enable someone to say something bad about you. In the politics and big egos of the corporate world, I remain professional at all times. When I need to blow (not that I can remember needing to do this for quite a while now) I would go for a walk, go to a café and then come back calmer. When there are things that need to be cleared in the air with a colleague or boss, I would find a way of having a word in private with that person to say what I have to say. It always helps me to be able to say what I have to say otherwise I would 'suffocate'. Then, I am done with that 'thing', move on and get on with my work.

I take my roles seriously so when I am in my profession, I dress and look the part. When I am a mother, I look the part – my children will tell you; just a look would be sufficient to let them know to 'behave else...' when they were younger. When I am off duty from everything, I play the part – I am carefree, I behave like a child, I laugh, giggle, have 'tantrum' if I don't have my way. I am 'me' without responsibility. As a mother, I brought up my children in a different way, in the way that aligned with my upbringing as much as possible because being in a different country I had to adapt to certain things. From my eldest daughter, I used to get the eternal "why can x stay out at night until 10pm and I have to be home at 8pm?" my eternal answer "because you are my daughter and x is not" – "why can't I shave my legs?", "why can't I have a tattoo?". Well, I was over the moon when my daughter was finally independent and I could relinquish the responsibility of making those decisions for her to fit my standards. She can now shave every part of her body and fill every inch of her skin with tattoos. Phew... what a relief!

When I am told I am different, I take pride in it. Rebekha, my daughter, labels me as being 'extra' all the time. It is all subjective anyway. Your way and my way are two different ways and both are fine.

I am naturally high. I get excited easily, I get chatty and I get merry. My cheeks even get rosy like when I drink wine. I do not need drugs or alcohol. My state of balance is being happy and positive and in the present. My state is key to me and it is influenced by many components – my sleep primarily, my diet, the activities I am engaged with, my environment and who I am immediately surrounded by. What I read, what I watch, what I listen to also contribute. I am very friendly and sociable and, at the same time, I love my own company and I love being surrounded by silence. I have not had a TV for many years now, about eight years and that was the best thing ever. I do not read newspapers and I do not listen to general news. I like to hear positive and inspiring news. There are so many inspiring videos on YouTube that actually give me goose pimples when I watch them and they make my worries seem like a tiny speck of dust. I know that there are a lot of bad stuff out there in the world and I do not need to read, see or hear about them for me to know that they exist.

Actually, there are some bad things out there that I do not even need to know because it does not lift me up. When I am in the company of someone who is regurgitating all the bad news out there, it lowers my state at the time. The funny thing about it is that some people have to share those news with someone and they would not take 'no' for an answer. When I am with such people, I just switch off and do not partake in the energy that is being shared about such news. Give me good news and I will be agitated, excited and happily share my energy back. In the times when the children were growing up and I had challenges with raising them and with my relationship, I would have to meditate and visualise regularly. Now, I do not even need to do that because I jealously guard my space and energy against anything and anyone that does not serve my purpose of balance.

I do not get attached to things and people – not even my children. I love them, I miss them when they are far from me, I have concerns about their safety and their wellbeing and that is about it. I do not spoil my grand-daughter. I remember saying to someone that I do not intend to spoil Ly'ora and the person replied "oh you will... you will see". Well I do not. I have the same strictness with her as I did with her mother. Why would I give her sweets and fizzy drinks when I did not give these to my children. Do I love her less that I do not care about her wellbeing as much as I cared for my children? I do not understand this concept of grand-parents spoiling their grand-children.

Everything that I do, I do it through choice. The choice might be heavily influenced by society, the way I have been brought up, my fears, my beliefs and my values; however, I always ponder why I should do it and then decide. Sometimes my daughter asks me to babysit my grand-daughter and I do not really want to, so I make a calculation in my head and then I decide. If, however, I have other plans then there is no need to calculate and I just refuse without feeling guilty about it. Guilt, this is another interesting topic...let's explore this in the next section...

Stand Out Free-style Notes

- Who do you want to be?
- Do you know the rules of engagement for the situations and environment around you – where to merge, when to stand out, how to gel?

Judgment/Guilt/Regrets

Your business is my business

Ahhh... guilt....so sweet... the weapon of 'love'. "Oh, but I did this for you last time, won't you do this for me this time". "I sacrificed for you all these years, I brought you onto this world and now I need you to put your life on hold and look after me"... well it is not said like this but you get the meaning of it.

In the name of love, I hold you responsible to looking and taking care of me when I am old... or sometimes not even when I am old but right now.... I have given you the best years of my life and now you are leaving me for so and so...

Regrets and guilt are two companions that I never care to have in my company. Anything that I have done, I have done to the best of what I could do at the time. If I had to go through the same experience again, would I maybe behave differently and make a different decision? – surely yes for some of them. But at the time, that was my best. So I forgive myself although, truly, I never have anything to forgive myself about. If I can forgive myself as such, can I forgive another person? Surely yes. He/she did the best at the time, so again nothing to forgive. It sounds simplistic and it is though it is not as simple as 'I forgive you and now all is ok'. At the end of the day, I relate everything back to me and I work on myself until I can be in a healthy place of no regrets or guilt.

I study human nature, I study my nature – I am human after all just like everyone else. I learn about the characteristics of human nature and then I deal with everyone as individuals. That helps me cast no judgment whenever I can. I am someone who is 'selfishly' more interested in my business than yours. So whenever I catch myself in someone else's business, I take myself back to my point of interest which is my business. Byron Katie, the author of "A Thousand Names for Joy", says it well 'Whose business are you in? God's business, the other's business or your business?' If I am anywhere except my business, what am I doing there? I am certainly trespassing.

As a mother, I get pulled into my children's business many times – it is an instinct thing. When I regain awareness, I brush my hands off and I leave their business. Hey, I am busy enough in my own to find the time to be in others'.

Live and let live is another motto that I like. I may make the judgment that people need me to save them or teach them manners or educate them.... Not in my job description. Who am I to think that I am better than them or that they cannot cope without my help? That would be arrogant of me. As mentioned in this book, I make changes in me first and everyone else benefits through the rippling effect of the waves and energy. So I judge that I need to save me, I need to teach me manners and I need to educate me. That's as far as I can pass the buck. I would say "you make me angry"... how can someone make me angry? Really? That is silly. What? They come over, do some funny thing for me to feel the heat rise from my toe to the tip of my hair, then they do some other magic to make my face change, the middle vein on my forehead to swell up, my eyes to narrow and spit fire and for me to feel the shakes of rage taking over my whole body???!!!!! Be real now. Who would have so much power over me like that if it is not 'moi' (i.e. me)! I like that – you make me sad, you make me cry, you make me laugh, you make me miss my sentence.... You, you, you, you. I am reclaiming my power and I am making it me, me me! I am making me cry, I am making me angry, I am making me laugh. I do make myself laugh actually. I look at myself in the mirror and pull faces at myself. I look at my grey hair that is fashionably growing only on one side of my head and I laugh at it. How can it not be funny this play of life that I am acting in? How can I not laugh at how my closest and dearest know exactly what strings to pull to spring me into a reaction... even my charming young grand-daughter knows exactly what to do to get my attention.

I was not always like this, enjoying life and letting things be. My friends say that I have a healthy attitude to life and I just take it as it comes. What else can I do? If I cannot control the rain, why would I get upset if it rains? I was certainly a hot head when I was younger, specially, when I was at university looking after my two young children, then afterwards when I was making my place in the professional and financial world. Some years later, my third child came on the scene and, juggling everything around, I used to take everything seriously, life, people, problems, money... you name it. I used to frequently jump on my high horse. I used to get upset when people would mis-spell my first name – how dare they not take close notice of how to write/say my name. Thinking about who I was then, it is funny. I used to be someone who had to convince people of my ideas, who would make noise if something was not fair in my view, who would be making things happen, who knew better, who had to be heard above everyone else... Well some people perceived my non-passive personality as bordering aggressive, imposing and bossy. So I have toned it down with awareness. When in groups, I sometimes deliberately remain quiet so others can take initiatives. My study of astrology and NLP (Neuro Linguistic Programming) has given me insights of the various types of people and this has helped me tremendously when leading and influencing others. I would understand why this team member required a lot of affirmations and confirmations of what needed to be done whereas with another team member all I needed to do was give a clear brief of what is required and he would run with it.

Awareness and choice – choosing what to do, what to say... when I choose, whether I am choosing the right or wrong thing, it is my choice and I deal with the consequence because I made the choice in the first place. It enables me to take responsibility for everything. I cannot blame someone else and it does not give me the choice to hide behind 'they' or 'us' or 'he' or 'she'.

In the days that I had any judgment, guilt or regret, I would observe it, analyse it, analyse how I felt and why, and bring some logic into it. If I was still emotional about it, I would park it until I could tackle it with less emotion. I used to look at my colleagues who did not have any dependents and who were earning similar or more money than me. I used to think, wow, how life would be sweet financially if did not have to provide everything all by myself for my children. If I did not have the children to provide for would my life have been sweeter? Would it? Who would I be then? Without every encounter that I had in my past, I would not be who I am today. I know that without all (every single one) challenges that I have come across, I would not have expanded so much in my self-awareness and self-development. As painful as it was, I am grateful for each of those challenges and everyone who has contributed to them.

Judgment Guilt Regrets Free-style Notes

- Whose business are you constantly or frequently in that is not your own?
- Who is in your business who should not be there?
- What do you wish to do about it?

Au Naturel (Natural)

Close to Mother Nature

Let's get to the pragmatic side now. So far in the book, it has been about the inner me, the attributes, traits values and beliefs that are components of me. Now it is more the pragmatic side of things. I have this section here because I am a whole – everything counts. I do not ignore any part of me. So let's begin.

Food

I love food. I do not like meat but I love meat with bones. I go through phases of not eating meat at all and I have always loved fish and eaten fish. However, a couple of months ago, I sort of have gone off fish too. I do not beat myself up about food. I would like to change my figure and I have a target in mind which is not related to what society says is ideal based on my body frame and height but it is based on what makes me comfortable and feel good. The suit that I was wearing when I celebrated my 40th birthday many years ago still fits me. The cloth is a bit frayed in between the legs but otherwise it is as good (almost) as new. So my figure has been fairly constant.

I love fine dining and fine wine though I am 'gone' usually after one glass of wine or champagne. My daughter and I were celebrating our business venture yesterday and I had a 'bisou bisou' which, in French, means 'kiss kiss'. It was the name of a champagne cocktail and I was certainly quite merry after that one glass. So I am afraid that my days of fine wine are on a countdown.

So, I do not generally eat a lot of meat. Vegetables or grains are prominent in my day to day meal. When I was growing up in a family of five children and my parents, my Mum would cook a pound (in weight) of beef cut into small pieces with vegetables and we would eat this with rice, all seven of us which included my Dad and my two older brothers who all had very good appetites. I remember my Mum would even count the pieces to ensure we all had equal share which, I guess, was based on how old/big we were. Of course, my Dad would have the better share being the sole bread winner of the household. Sometimes my Mum would even put some away so that my brothers could take with them to work the next day.

I have brought up my children in a similar way where I would use fresh vegetables most of the time. I would come from work, cook, then we would eat and that was the evening nearly over. I would generally cook several vegetables as well as some meat or fish on a Sunday. When we were only three of us, my oldest two children and me, I would buy a whole chicken and make three dishes out of it. I would use the legs, thighs and wings to cook some curry with potatoes and vegetables and eat with rice. I would use the chicken breast to use in fried rice or noodles and then I would have the rest left over to make some soup or some other dishes. These were simple days. Then they got bigger, the family grew with the addition of my youngest daughter and so I had to cook bigger portions.

My take on food is to stick to nature as much as possible. I eat organic and free range whenever I can and I give my system a rest regularly in the summer by juicing for a few consecutive days. In winter, my body is too cold to enjoy the goodness of juicing so I don't push it. I come from an island where there are multi races, so my cuisine varies between Indian, Muslim, French influenced and local dishes. Since coming to England, I have added Caribbean, African, English, Italian and other cuisines to the choices of dishes that I cook. So, I am never short of cooking up something.

More recently, since finding out about my grand-daughter's nut/ peanut allergy and various food intolerances, my daughter, Rebekha, and I have been finding ways to cook and bake without gluten, wheat, dairy, soya, eggs or nuts. We tend to cook something that we can all eat including Ly'ora so that she is included in everything. Rebekha has spent hundreds of hours – I am not exaggerating here – in researching and cooking/baking alternatives that are almost like for like to our everyday food. To us, it is not about taking the shortcut, it is about always taking the better and healthier route.

Skin

Same theme here. I do not follow brands, I do not follow fads, I follow nature. I moisturise my legs with almond oil. I use a face cream that is not full of chemicals and I have been using the same one for years. If it works, why change it? I do not use anti-ageing anything. In fact, just seeing that word on anything puts me off it even if it is the best product in the world. Why would I need anti-ageing? I want to age with my age! Where I come from, growing old is not an issue and it is a natural and beautiful phenomenon. Also, getting married and having children was a natural progression to growing up too. Hence I have never been torn between my career and being a mother. I never had to decide when is the right time to have my children. When I had them that was the time.

So skin wise, I do not cream my body purely because I do not like the feeling of grease (oiliness) on my hands and arms etc. My legs and feet, I do not have a choice (almost) otherwise I would be walking around with "grey skin" as my daughter Rebekha would put it. So I grease them just enough to keep them in check and not enough for the oiliness to bother me.

Hair

For many years, I would blow dry my hair each time I washed it. Then my oldest daughter introduced me to ways of drying and maintaining my hair naturally. She herself had gone natural after relaxing and heating her hair for many years and ending up with hair thinning and breakage. She then researched and perfected her way of keeping her hair healthy 'au naturel' meaning natural. Here is another example of problem solving naturally and something positive resulting from a challenge in our life. She has now influenced so many people around her into keeping natural hair.

I was used to having sleek and wavy hair. Working in the city, the sleek hair fitted well with the City working with the high heels, designer suits etc. I felt good and I was comfortable in my skin. Then I tried the natural hair style which resulted in my hair being freezy curly. I kept feeling that it was messy because with naturally curly hair, bits of hair are always sticking out. I felt that the hair style was clashing with my City Sleek professional. Then I found some hairstyles which kept the hair more tamed and therefore more in line with my image. Eventually, I have grown so used to my natural hair now that I would not feel as comfortable having the sleek blow dried hair and having to care for it. I use natural products to wash and condition my hair and almond oil has been my hair moisturiser for ever, for as long as I can remember, from the days that I was still living in my homeland.

Just like with my view on anti-ageing products, I am not torn between 'to dye or not to dye'… my hair that is. I told a friend that I do not intend to dye my hair and she replied "of course you will, you need to". I smile at such comments. Why do I need to? I have seen friends and relatives struggling with keeping up the hair dyeing process. I have seen people where their roots are grey from not having had time to go and cover up on time. Don't be mistaken, for those that like to dye their hair that is fine with me. It is all about what makes someone look comfortable and confident within herself. With me, I am as comfortable as ever with my grey hair. I am too impatient to take on the hassle of having my hair dyed.

You will notice that the recurring theme through this section is 'natural'!

Health

I believe that due to the healthy life style I had in Mauritius, my health has been quite good through the years since I moved to England. There were not many cars in Mauritius in those days so it was mainly travelling by buses and walking a lot. Children would play outside all the time and there was always some outdoor activities to take part in. My early life style carried me over into my adult years.

Once I turned 50, I decided that it was time to give my system a boost to carry it over the remaining years. So I am even more mindful of what I eat and drink and I try (I say try) to incorporate some physical exercises in my daily life. Sometimes it happens, sometimes it does not but the intention is there....

I do not automatically take medication for any illness that I have. I research what I am prescribed paying particular attention to side effects. I aim for preventative remedies and alternative therapies as much as possible.

Rebekha had a condition when she was about 6-8 years old where she would have regular tummy pain. We went from one consultation to the other until finally the doctor advised to operate on her to investigate the cause of the pain. The intervention required a long funnel shaped metal tube to be inserted into her anal passage and a telescope inserted into the metal funnel (shall we call it) to peek at what is going on there. They mentioned that she was quite young to have that intervention and would ensure they use a smaller size and length funnel. Hey, I ran in the opposite direction! Well not literally. At the time, she was really in pain and I had to think about it and decide. I thought about it hard and could not imagine my daughter having that "thing" up her "derriere" (as we say in French) so I declined. I decided to explore the alternative therapy route first and found a lady in

West London that did reflexology. For months, I would take Rebekha all the way from Walthamstow, East London, where we lived at the time to West London to have a weekly session. It was not cheap and I do not even know how I funded this treatment. Result, the pain disappeared. Many people do not believe in using alternative therapies. For me it worked and spared Rebekha feeling the funnel and that is more than good enough.

Similarly, Jasmine developed vocal nodules when she was about 3-4. The doctors did not have any solution for us except operating on her. The consultant that would perform the operation informed us that Jasmine would be the youngest person that he had operated on. Well, I pondered and pondered and declined the option. In the end the vocal nodules were cured by Jasmine following speech therapy sessions that gave her exercises that taught her how to use her voice to enable her throat to heal.

I am always looking for some other ways to resolve a challenge, a way that aligns with me and that is gentle and not intrusive.

Exercise
Well, exercise, not much more to add really. This is lacking and this is an area of my life that I need to improve on just because I want to. When I feel like it, I will get to the gym and work hard, when I do not feel like it, then....

I do not beat myself about it. In fact, I do not beat myself about anything. Everything has a place and a reason to happen and it happens whether I want to or not. There is nothing else to it.

In the earlier days when the children were young and my life was stressful, I used yoga, meditation and visualisation to help me get through life. Nowadays I do not need these tools to keep me in sync and balanced.

"Au Naturel" Free-style Notes

- What is your take on your food, skin and health?
- Do you give yourself the best that you can because you 'deserve it'?
- What improvements do you wish to add to your existing routine?

Congruence

True to Myself

This is my final topic. It is sort of the conclusion of this book. I choose not to call it 'Conclusion'.

What makes a difference in my life, what makes me loved by my children, is that I live by my rules, motto, views etc. I do as I say. I motivate them, help them, boost them up even when I really don't want to or they are getting on my nerves, which they do. I also tell them off and turn away from them if they are doing something that is seriously not aligned to me as a person and I am frank with them about it. I do not judge them. My youngest used to say (maybe she was just teasing me) that one day she would have a house where the walls inside are painted black. She would then ask "will you come to see me Mummy?" and I would reply "I would come to see you and we would meet up in a café near your home and I would not come inside your house". I was not joking when I said that. Dark colours pull me down. All my children are now adults and, for me, it is a big responsibility that I do not carry anymore – they can make their own choices! I might not like the choice, I might not agree with the choice but I do not have to live with their choice because it is their life. If asked, I will tell them what I think of the choice and then let them be.

No matter who is around me in my life, I do everything I can to remain true to myself. For this to happen, I need to know myself in a pretty good way.

I do not offend someone deliberately, I follow society's rules where needed and, where not needed, I follow my own rules. Sometimes

I follow the crowd because I get swamped into the waves or it is convenient but I would come out and realign myself constantly, more and more. When I start a new habit, for example when I was training myself not to lose my temper so quickly, many times I would flip and remember afterwards that I should have slowed my breathing down, taken deep breaths, etc. Eventually, I would remember this during the act of losing my temper (and most of the time it would be too late to put them in practice) and then one day I would remember this before I would lose my temper. I would recognise the signs that would be leading up to me losing my temper such as my body responses, my thoughts, my breathing and I would then implement what I needed to before my volcanic temper erupted. Where am I going with this?

It is about me and always about me and my task is ensuring that I am true to myself while allowing others to be true to themselves. Is it about them? No, it is still about me giving others respect, space and allowing them to be different to me. Do I need to understand them always? No! Why do I need to understand them? I am me and they are them! How can a pea understand a carrot? If I cannot understand someone, I just need to accept the person as who he or she is. What is so difficult about this? Do I need all my loved ones to understand me? No way! Just accept me or do not accept me. First though, I need to accept myself as I am, with all my flaws and all my battles and all my beauty. It makes the whole.

I do not try to convince people about my views. Why should I? If I was a politician, maybe I would have to because I need all these followers otherwise I would suck at being a politician. I am not a politician. I know the roles that would fit me well and those that would not. Like working with children, you are joking... I am in awe of people who genuinely enjoy (I mean really enjoy and it is not just a job) working with children. I have just about made the 'Pass' mark with my own children, let alone other peoples' children.

So all in all, it is me in front of a mirror reflecting back at me!

Congruence Free-style Notes

- How are you congruent in your life?
- How do you remain true to yourself?
- Look at yourself in your mirror – are you happy with what you see/feel? If not, change something.

Wrapping Up

My final words (... for now)

My life has progressively become easier and easier as I have 'graduated' through the tough classes of this school called Earth. I put it down to the fact that I do learn my lessons when I get kicked and I do something different so that I do not get the same kick again. Hey, I may get another type of kick but not that same one again. No, thank you. Of course, being financially stable, having young adult children, being in mature relationships with everyone close to me helps make my life smoother. I am referring here about my attitude on life as a whole, my mindset and my interactions with others. If I have to sum it up, I would say that I now take it easy. I do not try to change another person, I do not try to take on the world, I do not try to fix the problems of the world. I only fix myself. I give advice when I am asked to, I shut up when I am not asked (well most of the time) and, as much as possible, I give others the power to discover how strong they can be and how amazing they can be. This is my religion and spirituality.

I am very careful of the environment that I put myself in. If my personal space and environment at home is not giving me the energy that I need, I change my surroundings. If I am in an environment where I do not have any control over it and I am not comfortable, I get myself out of it as soon as I can. My environment impacts my mindset, my mindset impacts my feelings, my feelings impact my behaviour and my behaviour impacts everything and everyone that I 'touch'. It is like a circular domino effect. One little thing impacts the whole thing.

I am careful who I let into my external and internal environment. I am mindful who I spend time with. Some people I can only take in small dosage and usually life arranges everything so that I do not have to spend more time than needed with them

I would say that I am in a good place. I do not need to impress anyone. I do not need anyone to impress me. I am not a millionaire or a billionaire. If I am one day then that is fine, if I am not then that is fine too. My goals are not just about money or just about health or just about this or that, my goals link everything together. I have recently experienced what it feels like to be passionate about an idea, a goal and this is an amazing experience. This happened with my daughter Rebekha and we were both 'breathing in one breath' together so to speak. It was more than amazing.

I do not have to live life anymore, I let life live me and each step along the way, I am finding magical things and magical people and it is still all about me.

This book is about being who I am and putting it out there to inspire others to be who they truly are. There are no rules but one, 'be true to myself'. Will someone judge me and see something 'wrong' with me? You bet! That is fine with me. Will someone find something useful in this book? Yes and that is really fine with me. If nothing else, my children will learn a few more things about me that they did not know about already and they will find a few more reasons to call me 'extra'! That is certainly fine with me.

Love is everywhere, and I just have to become aware and let it in.

Wrapping Up Free-style Notes

- What is your story?
- How about writing a book?
- How about baring it all and dropping the pretense? Think about it! Email me and I will guide you on getting it done.

Freedom of Speech

How others perceive me

In this section, I allow space for my children, the three people who have been with me all their life, who know me best and who have shared the journey with me through thick and thin (almost literally) to write down how they perceive me as a person, a mother, a friend (maybe), an advisor, a teacher and a disciplinarian.

I also provide a space for my siblings and others who have known me, some for a long time, others not, to also write down what they think I am about from the interaction I have with them and how I have touched their life (if at all).

I am always interested to hear what others have to say about me as long as they are being totally honest and not coerced into saying what they think would please me.

In line with the 'free style' and 'bare all' theme of this book, nothing that is written in the section will be edited and I will ensure my book editor remains clear of this section.

This list features my children first followed by my siblings and then feedback from some of my friends in strict order in which I received each 'bio'.

This process of getting feedback from others has been an extraordinary experience with almost a surreal feel to it. I feel privileged and humbled to have been able to know what others genuinely think about me.

My Multi-Talented, oh so loving, Youngest Daughter – 31st January 2016

So my profile of Mum is going to be quite short and concise, as I feel that she is that type of individual in reality; the type who gets straight to the point and quite frankly is deathly allergic to any sort of waffling or mastication.

I don't really know how to describe Mum as the minute you try and put her into a pigeon hole she begins to wriggle and struggle with all her might to defy its criteria. You could call her eccentric in the way she lives; without a TV and the way she wishes to return to the age where people actually socialised with each other face to face, and aren't bent over a screen of some sort.

Furthermore she is the free-est spirit you will ever meet. She does, however, follow her own pattern and rhythm and has an obvious centre making her a reliable and sturdy source to gain perspective and advice from; even if it is the most cut throat advice you will hear, you will receive no fluff or sugar coating but the absolute truth and fact; (which I personally find advantageous since you will know what you need to know within the first 10 minutes of the conversation).

In conclusion I don't really know why I'm trying to summarise Mum's character within this measly paragraph as it is an impossible task, as is trying to describe the ocean to someone who has only ever seen land. Nevertheless here are bunch of words that kind of ISH describe her; Different, Honest, Considerate, Loving, Brutal, Straightforward, Youthful, Wise, Short Fused, Patient, Impatient, Powerful, Unsympathetic but Caring, Motivational and A Role Model! If I am to be honest you will just have to experience her yourself to truly grasp the individual known to me as MUM ☺.

* * * * * * * * *

My Rebellious, mirror of me, Eldest Daughter – 2nd February 2016

Marie-Anne has known me for all 27 years of my life, however I can only say that I have truly know Marie-Anne for the better part of 6-7 years if even that. Both Marie-Anne and I have been to hell and back and this is putting our journey lightly. In the beginning I remember us being like best friends, even sisters when I close my eyes and recall the blurry images from my past. In my teenage years we butted heads (I can't help but wonder if this is to do with me being a Taurus, an almighty bull) and for a year life forced us apart for what I now appreciate as a separation that was much needed for our internal growth back towards one another. It was the beginning of a journey we continue to take in this journey as we choose (depending on our thoughts) to float or struggle through the river of life. I have and very often still choose to struggle on my journey through life. It is on these occasions that I (always) stubbornly turn to Marie-Anne feeling hopeless, drained, exhausted, and, every time I have reached my hand out desperately asking and needing help she has had the right words, been available at the right times, been the neutral emotionally unattached yet comforting, understanding teacher I have always needed. We are similar and yet very different and it is because we are two sides of the same coin that I respect and cherish what she offers at my table when in need because she has unique views, opinions and methods from my own that have always led me to my solution if not immediately then indirectly and eventually. She is not just my mother and my best friend, she is my adviser, and most importantly my enemy because those that care don't give you what you want, they give you what you need and this she has always done. Without her I would have no business, I would have given up as a mother, I would have beaten myself up for my failures, I would still hold grudges. Without Marie-Anne I wouldn't be one of the few that sees the positive in all situation. It's always there if you just bother to look. With universal love Rebekha Gooden – the problematic middle child

* * * * * * * * *

58

My Unique, with that gorgeous dimple, Son – 3rd February 2016

Since I was young my mum was a single parent, very career focused. At that time there were just three of us, Rebekha and myself Reuben. We were not the easiest of kids to have so as you can imagine my mum was extremely strict. I remember living in a hostel, the three of us while we went to school and she worked a full time job and studied at university. It obviously started paying off as we then moved in to a two bedroom flat then a much larger flat in Forest Gate where my younger sister Jasmine was born until we moved to what would be our family home in Walthamstow East London just before I started secondary school. Things were as you can imagine very tight and hard, a single mother of three working full time as well as trying to raise three kids to the best she can. Being influenced by people at school my sister and I were very bad and a lot of hard work, I remember being kicked out to live with my dad multiple times as well as being driven to the police station as a scare tactic. As the years went on, as we got older, I did notice my sisters being treated a lot more different then me and I started to resent this and wonder why. After a few years past and I by now had become a man my mum finally told me she had treated my sisters different as they were female and didn't want them to ever rely on a man and to be independent. It made sense to me finally and I saw things my mum started doing for me that made me think she feels bad for giving my sisters more attention than me and was trying to make up for it. As the years went on we had our ups and downs but she has always gone from strength to strength starting from a normal job living in a hostel with kids to now owning two houses, land in Birmingham, very high up in her career, a mentor, writes books to help others, CEO in the new family business venture. The family has become very close same as her career and mindset now.

* * * * * * * *

59

My sister Marie France – 1st February 2016

I am Marie-Anne's sister. I know her as a 'simple'* and coura-geous woman who has had to deal with difficulties in her life and who has subsequently overcome them. Today I am proud of her. Continue little sister. God bless you.

*Note: 'simple' in French means unpretentious / unassuming.

Marie France
Mauritius

* * * * * * * * *

My sister Claudie – 2nd February 2016

I have only good things to say about Marie-Anne. Not only because she is my sister, but she is really great. I am the eldest sister and she is the youngest but sometimes it may seem the contrary. When I am down, she is the one who lifts me up. She is there for everyone who needs her. She has been there when I had to cope with Mam's illness (Alzheimers) who was staying with me. She was there when I was not well after Mam's death and so many other times. She is a fighter and she gives her strength to those who are in contact with her. There is so much to say but I think that what I said before resumes well the kind of person she is.

En resumé, Marie-Anne is the one who will always 'stand by you' whenever needed.

Claudie
Mauritius

* * * * * * * * *

My brother Pierre – 6th February 2016

Marie-Anne has taught me to be self-confident, how to enjoy life again and never to lose courage. To never give up, how to implement my values. She always gives me good advice. Marie-Anne has always been a go-getter. For me, her brother, she is a heroine.

I wish you best wishes for the future.

Pierre
Mauritius

* * * * * * * * *

Katie – 28th January 2016

I met Marie-Anne Rasé five years ago at a convention in New York. It's funny how life unfolds, you never know from moment to moment who you will meet, connect with, and even develop a life-long friendship with. Well, my ten minute conversation with Marie-Anne turned into a lasting friendship that spans time, distance (I live in the US, she lives in the UK), cultural backgrounds, and life experiences. However, these superficial differences have only added to the humor, laughter and love we share as friends. Marie-Anne has a passion and inexhaustible energy to help others fulfill their potential, and in doing so, she naturally fulfills her own. She is many things to many people, but beyond the roles of being a – sister, mother, grandmother, wife, business woman, mentor and coach – she is first and foremost a friend to the people in her life. Marie-Anne, thank you for your friendship, and now, as my dad would say, "Sock it to 'em!!"

Katie Murphy
Human Resources Professional
North Carolina, USA
28/01/2016

* * * * * * * * *

Laurianne – 30th January 2016

My name is Laurianne, I emigrated to the UK sixteen years ago in search of new pastures for a better life. I had education and learning in mind. I am a specialist preoperative practitioner and have worked in critical care for the past 33 years.

I am fifty -seven years old and I still work part time in theatres. I am currently studying because I believe my purpose in life has not quite finished. I feel deep inside me a need to explore myself and give back all the wisdom, expertise and experience accumulated over the years.

Marie-Anne fits in very well in the picture of an enabler. I met Marie about 14 to 15 years ago. We happened to be from the same country but we became friend when I moved to the UK. I brought a parcel from the island for her daughter's holy communion and she rescued Jacques' mom when we forgot to pick her up from Heathrow airport. Marie is somebody of integrity there is no two ways about it. She will always endeavour to do what is right no matter the cost or the distance.

We have grown to love and respect each other.

Without even having to think about it, I will say Marie is a natural guru. She mentors naturally without thinking about it, she is an enabler in the sense that she does not direct you but simply and gently point you in the right direction. She never judges or tell you what to do. She has self-awareness and will share her experience and time with you without expecting anything back in return.

She is an energiser and has been a role model for me many times in my life. I believe Marie-Anne has had a plate full of difficult situations in her life, but she always has looked on the bright side and make positive choices. I am inspired by this woman positive ways of sorting everyday life, she observes and listens and this makes her a special person. She has been a little gem in my life when life gets rough and confusion sets in for me, I can rely on a phone call or a visit to London to my good friend, I always come back energised not because Marie has told me what to do but because she has listened and genuinely empathised with her old friend. Time and time again she has let me come up with my own answer by being there for me, she has help me to rise again and again and it takes a good nature to do this.

Marie rides the waves of life with confidence and gentleness and I am so proud to be part of her life and her achievements.

Yours sincerely
Laurianne
Leeds

* * * * * * * *

Tracy – 31st January 2016

"There is no such thing as coincidence", says Marie-Anne." Our paths cross for a reason!"

And how right that has proven to be. We worked at the same large charity in London for many years before a 'chance' meeting on a training course. That was 20 years ago and we have become firm friends ever since.

The training course helped launch my journey of self-discovery. That may sound grandiose, but it's just another way of saying how I want to create a life that is happy and balanced. That journey is one that is full of ups and downs, opportunities to reflect on events and my response to them. Marie-Anne has been brilliant at helping to clarify my thinking when I have come up against situations that have clouded my judgement.

Last year, my husband died very suddenly and unexpectedly. I experienced behaviour from his family that completely threw me and put me in a tail spin. Marie-Anne was full of compassion and understanding, but did not buy into the story of 'the in laws should not have behaved like this. Why did they not show me any compassion? Why don't they call to ask how I am? How could they do this to me?'

Marie-Anne just asked the simple question: "what did you expect?"

That brought me up with a start! Although initially I didn't like the question, I began to think about it. I realised that if I held on to the expectations, then I suffered. I was upset and making myself ill. I realised that however I responded to what I first saw as hurtful behaviour, it had no effect whatsoever on the family. But I was affected. I couldn't eat. I couldn't sleep. When I realised this, I understood how crazy it was. Why would I *choose* to make myself ill?

I know that whenever I need an outside perspective that I can turn to Marie-Anne for insight and powerful coaching.

When coached by Marie-Anne it is impossible not to feel her full attention focused on you and your issue. It is like a powerful spotlight that reveals the alternative view of a situation and response. Her coaching is given with tremendous compassion; it is gentle yet incisive and clear. Her gift is knowing what to say and how, so that her client can hear her wisdom.

She lives her life in a way that is totally inspiring. When I think of Marie-Anne, I see a woman of amazing strength and energy, who walks tall, full of grace and calm. When she smiles, her whole face lights up. She touches everyone that she meets.

Tracy
Portugal

* * * * * * * *

J. Manji – 2nd February 2016

I first met Marie-Anne over 2 years ago when she joined the company I worked for at the time. I had just moved into a Business Analyst position after being a MI (Management Information) Analyst there for 8 years. I was working on a different project to Marie-Anne and I can't recall how we started speaking whether it was to do with work or just friendly chat but I remember at the time I knew she was someone I would get on very well with and I was right.

I often ask her for advice on Business Analysis given her extensive knowledge and experience and she has this incredible ability to explain anything in a simple structured way and always gives me that confidence I need or more likely a kick up the backside ha ha.

I don't know many people like her, she has this get-up-and-go attitude no matter what's going on around her, the juggling work life with home life and then social life and if anyone has a full on out of work life it is Marie-Anne but she takes it all in her stride. I feel like the 50+ old compared to her!

Marie-Anne is supportive, helpful, considerate, understanding, motivating (the list goes on and on) and who would think she is a Bollywood film fan and specifically loves Mr SRK lol.

She has definitely helped me with where I am now, new job, new experiences and increased confidence in my own abilities. If she took on a BA mentoring job I would be first in line for sure.

I am so fortunate to have met Marie-Anne, a great friend; it was fate that we both ended up working for the same company again.

J. Manji
Business Analyst
London, UK

* * * * * * * *

Sabrina – 3rd February 2016

Whenever I think about Marie Anne, it's her radiant smile, distinctive to combative women that first come to my mind. Yes! At first sight, her severe look, can impress, but it should not be misinterpreted. Marie Anne is a woman who knows what she wants and needs. Above all she is not the kind of person to beat around the bush. She has struggled enough in life to know that it's pointless to waste time in any situation. Though, I can say that I have known Marie Anne, since ever (from family), because I have mostly heard about her, I really met her in November 2014, during a visit in UK. Today, I can say that I feel privileged to be in touch with Marie Anne. I admire the self-made and independent woman she is, living a value-based life and enjoying the least simple thing that can bring joy and happiness.

Sabrina
Mauritius

****

Brigitte – 3rd February 2016

It is Brigitte from Mauritius. I am very happy to have met Marie-Anne. I feel very comfortable with her. She triggers something within me. Since I have spoken to Marie-Anne, I have gained more self-confidence, I get a lot, a lot. I feel I have grown.

Brigitte
Mauritius

****

Jacqueline – 3rd February 2016

Marie-Anne is an intelligent and determined woman. She has had to struggle by herself and in spite of the many difficulties, she has come out of them. Even in the midst of her problems, she has kept a firm head on her shoulders. She had to find solutions all by herself in the many challenges of her life and she has been able to learn the best lessons from those various experiences. She leads all her projects till their complete achievement and does not make hasty decisions.

Jacqueline
Mauritius

****

Almost last but not least – "Thiérry" – 4th February 2016

'Rasé', 'MA', 'Ma Vieille' (French for 'Old Girl')...all aliases I have used over the past 6+ years, but have only used 'Marie-Anne' for about 1 week. I mean, honestly, life is too short for double barrelled first names! This is testament to her loveable, accepting and endearing character.

We first met working on an insurance claims transformation programme and have remained good friends ever since. Whilst perhaps not the most likely pairing of friendship, we continue to take time out to catch up over a meal on a regular basis. Rasé is accepting and manages to find a common ground with all walks of life, probably thanks to her open mind, acceptance of people and diverse interests – she's a borderline hippy at one end of the spectrum and professional businesswoman at the other end.

I have long admired MAs determined and action-orientated nature, having raised three loving kids (mostly as a single parent), all the while holding down a full-time job and somehow found time for studying for her University degree. In defiance of her advancing years (in spite of her looks, she's no spring chicken and is even a grandmother!) Rasé refuses to rest on her laurels and continues to lead a full and hectic life. Writing books, mentoring students, learning investment trading, starting up a specialist foods business with her eldest daughter, landlord, working full time as an IT contractor...all simultaneously

Ma Vieille – entrepreneur, writer, coach, mum, nan, wife...and my dear friend!

Terry
England

* * * * * * * * *

Jane – 5th February 2016
Marie-Anne came into my life when we were both escaping Save the Children. On a creative change course. Marie-Anne had such ambitious dreams very impressive with two children as a single parent along with a mischievous spirit and a capacity for laughter.

She was making her own path and taking everyone who wanted to along with her.

A great cook, a lover of life with a light touch.

I can't wait to see what the next chapter brings...

Jane xx

* * * * * * * * *

Carly – 6th February 2016
I've known Marie-Anne for nearly a year and a half, and I can honestly say, she is one of the most fair, selfless, caring people I know.

I grew to love her like a second mama when I lived with her, (she was my landlord) for a year.

She treated me like I was one of her own. Her energy is amazing. She uplifts, nurtures and guides without even knowing how big of an impact she's having. She has a huge heart and I believe she will take anyone under her wing.

Truly weird *cough* powdered baby formula *cough*, but even more wonderful. Her accent is the best, her laugh is hilarious, and her humour is, a little strange at times to say the least. I'm sure that we were meant to cross paths, because she has helped me in ways that I wouldn't even be able to describe.

She taught without even meaning to teach.

A very special woman indeed.

Carly Martin
London

* * * * * * * *

Rita – 18th February 2016
I have known Marie-Anne for almost 8 years now. We were initially colleagues and soon went on to become very good friends.

I have always looked on to Marie-Anne as my go-to person whenever things became difficult for me on personal front. There have been times when she was away on holiday and I spent ages trying to track her down to be able to speak to her.

She is a very strong personality, and is quite tough having been through a lot in her life. I can't even imagine how difficult raising three fine kids single handedly must have been. What makes her my go-to person is she is not judgemental. But neither is she scared to spell how out things the way they are. She is a good listener and I especially like the way she asks questions to make sure you have thought about all aspects of the problem. Apart from this, she is a fun loving person. You would never guess her age when you are with her!

I am so glad she is my friend. I wish her all the best with everything.

Rita
London

* * * * * * * * *

Clare – 26th February 2016
I met Marie-Anne at work. I was at a crossroads in my life, and was having a tough time both at work, and personally with my relationship with my daughter. Marie-Anne selflessly, lovingly and non-judgementally mentored me, and from her patience, caring nature and wisdom and approach, my life turned around and her positivity and advice greatly impacted my life.

To this day I believe Marie-Anne is a positive light, and was sent into my life to spiritually and mentally awaken me, and break chains which I felt could not be broken

Clare Harrington
London

* * * * * * * * *

Freedom of Speech Free-style Notes

- How do others perceive you?
- What do your loved ones have to say about you?
- How do you feel about what they say about you?
- What new things did you learn about yourself from feedback from others?

Reaching your Fulfilled
Self – Pull out Section

10 Most Significant Tips

This is the only section in this book where I will be directly talking to you, the reader, and share some tips.

If I was asked what are the 10 most important factors that have kept me youthful in mind, body and spirit I would share with others, it would be:-

1. <u>Know who you are</u> – not what someone else wants you to be, not copying someone you admire or being what you think society wants you to be, but truly what makes you tick, what inspires you, what energy elevates you, what takes you down, what are your weaknesses, what are your strengths, what you like about yourself, what you do not like… make it all about you. At first, you might not even be able to find out who you are because you would be so strongly associated with a role that you are playing. Pull each layer of a role off and persevere. Ask yourself questions such as "if I take away my thoughts, words and actions as a mother/ sister/wife/employee' (whichever role you perform) what is left?." You may then get to another role that you perform. Ask the same question and keep peeling the layers of your roles off one by one until you get to something – a kernel maybe – and maybe you might not even have words to describe that 'something' and that is ok. I call my kernel 'awareness' because for me

'awareness' does not have a body or a mother or children or a pet or a house or a car....

The next part is to love who you are. To love who you are, you need to accept who you are; accept the circumstances you were born in, accept the parents you have and the children you have. These you cannot change so just accept them. Then there are all the other people in your life and accept them too. If there is something that needs changing about the people around you, then, once you have accepted them, do something about it. People, circumstances, environments can be changed. I do not mean that they change for you but vice versa – you change for them. I do not mean you changing to become what others want you to be; what I mean you changing for you and, in doing so, you are changing for them in becoming who you are and along the way this may mean parting from old relationships and embracing new ones. When you change, others have to change. When your energy changes to the point that it does not match the environment and circumstances that you are in, those will change as well. Experiment for yourself.

2. <u>Take action</u> – when you are not happy about someone, something – maybe a situation – or even about yourself, do something about it. Keeping in 'it', whatever you are not liking, is not doing you any favors. It is possible that you are not able to do something about it immediately and you need time to build what is required for you to change the situation, then start the process of getting there. Just one step towards that process is an action. As an example, you might enjoy what you do in your job and you have an idea of a job that you would like to do but you do not have all the skills you need yet. Then look at the steps that you need to get you to that job – a step would be to look for courses that can give you the skills that you need, or find a friend that is already doing

73

the job that you want and who can mentor or coach you on getting there.

I am currently in the process of becoming a Master Practitioner of NLP (Neuro Linguistic Programming). When I was on the Foundation course, my trainer showed us the following principles of which, for me, underpins the art of taking action. Here is a high level summary of them:

a.   *Outcome* – know clearly in your mind the end result that is under your control that you want. What I mean by 'under your control', there is no point saying that your goal is for Jane, John or Jack to change… however, you can say that you want to improve yourself in this way or that way… to improve your relationship with Jane, John or Jack.

b.   *Sensory Acuity* – be aware of what is happening within you and outside you as a result of you taking action; people around you may respond in this way or that way or you may start feeling this way or that way. Be sensitive to that.

c.   *Flexibility* – based on the response that you are getting in the previous step and how close it is getting you to your outcome, adjust what you are doing or keep doing what you are doing. Maybe you might even want to change your outcome slightly or totally and that is all fine. Sometimes you might think you want X and when you get closer to X, you realise you want something else.

d.   *Rapport* – we live in society and cannot escape interacting with others. How do we get on with others? How much do others trust us? Rapport is about building the correct relationships with those around us – our children, our peers, our boss, our in laws, people we are doing business and negotiating with…

e.   *State Management* – underpinning all this, the state you are in is key. When I am low in energy, my

74

productivity level is reduced. When I am in a positive frame of mind, I can 'move mountains' so to speak; everything is possible and I get through completing a lot of tasks effortlessly. Our state and the state of others matter.

Once you are clear about your outcome, get going and do something that will take you towards that action; no matter how small the step is, just do something.

■ *Keep going through the steps as an iterative loop until you reach your outcome.*

I found this model so simple yet so profound that I have become fascinated by it. I attended the Foundation course with my daughters and as soon as we got back home I started playing with this model on a very very small scale. It is fun. This is an example of how I use it to a small timeline. My youngest daughter Jasmine loves (I mean loooooooves pizza). So this would be our conversation:

- *Me*: "Daughter, what is the outcome for dinner?"
- *Daughter*: "Oooh, have pizza"
- *Me*: "What action do you need to take"
- *Daughter*: "Order the pizza"
- *Me*: "Ok, and how are you going to do that?"
- *Daughter*: "Find the phone number, phone the pizza place and order"
- *Me*: "Ok get going"

Daughter phones pizza place, puts in her order, gets excited (it was very obvious that she had taken the right action for her outcome) and impatiently waits for pizza to arrive and then tucks into said pizza.

■ I really have fun playing with this. If my outcome this morning is to be washed and dressed by 10am, it is a no brainer what I need to do. I might decide to change my outcome to stay in bed all day, in which case I will go through the model to ensure I stay in bed all day. As fun as this is, it is the same model and steps for outcomes that are across a longer time span and that are bigger than 'eating pizza' or 'having a shower'. Test it yourself.

3. Tame your Thoughts – your thoughts are just that – thoughts! They are not reality and you may believe them so much that your reality and thoughts become blurry. The most challenging time of my relationship with my daughter was when she was in her teens. I was working full time and would get home about 6pm. She would have finished school and would be out and get back home at midnight or later. I did not have a clue where she was, who she was with, what she was doing. My worst fears for my daughters had been them being attacked or raped. So it is the middle of the night, I had a long day at work, I have to wake up in the morning and work the next day and my daughter is not home yet. I cannot sleep and my thoughts go wild… "I am going to hear a knock on the door in a moment and I will see a policeman when I open the door and I will find out that my daughter has been found in a ditch somewhere… blah blah blah". Nightmare!!!! When these type of thoughts happened, I would distract myself to not think about it. How would I do that? I would reason with myself – "if it was to happen there is nothing I can do at this moment in time, I will not worry about it until I know it has happened and until then I will trust that the Universe is taking care of my child. If I worry about it now it is not making my child safer and therefore what is happening is out of my control so I might as well not worry about it and get some form of sleep". Did it work? To a certain extent,

yes. The worry would be there but I would not be having those horrific thoughts of what was happening to my daughter. I do not fight the thoughts, I use my logical mind to reason about where best to channel my energy and what was best for me at that time, which obviously was getting some rest. Another typical example would be when I cannot get hold of my man when I expect to. His phone is switched off or unattainable. What????? Where is he? Who is he with? Blah blah blah. My mind goes racing that he is with another woman. So what do I do? I face that thought – so what if he is with another woman, how does that make me feel? I then acknowledge my feelings. This is not easy and it is a great process of me learning who I am. My next question would be – what would I do if he came back and told me he was with another woman? Again not easy. Sometimes, this would bring a reality check and make me realise that I love this man and I would 'prefer' not to lose him and so my attitude towards him may change and I may become even more loving, more understanding, more whatever.

I would have gone crazy if I had allowed my thoughts to run full territory with regards to my children or men. I am not joking. There are some crazy thoughts that sometimes, as soon as they surface, I acknowledge them and let them go away because they are so misaligned with who I am. If I allow these thoughts to be, they contradict me and I cannot afford for this to happen.

What is in your thoughts? Things will happen regardless of whether you worry about them or not. So why worry about something until it has happened.

The other aspect of this tip is to also <u>tame other people's thoughts</u>. You know those with good intentions that dump their experiences and project negativity on you. I cope with this by having an invisible shield and making a space between the person and me where those good intentioned thoughts/words can drop in and disappear. This is easy for me to do because I am totally clear that each person is different and has different views and ideas. I do not feel that I am obliged to agree and understand anyone and everyone except my children to a certain extent. Find your own way of taming other people's thoughts and not letting them come and join forces with your own thoughts.

4. <u>Keep Growing</u> – do not stop for one moment and think that you do not have anything else to learn. People fascinate me. I, being also a person, fascinate me. I did not plan to study NLP (Neuro Linguistic Programming) to such a degree. I took my daughters to the Foundation course to introduce my youngest (who had been too busy most of her young life studying, doing sports and doing art) to some form of self-development and communication skills. I believe that everyone needs self-development in life. So here I was on the Foundation course just to accompany my daughters and I got 'hooked'. The course was full of practical exercises and I took me by surprise. Yes you read correctly 'I' took 'me' by surprise meaning I surprised myself. I must also admit that the trainer was hilarious too and his training style rhymed with me. Now I am on my way to my Master's level. Why did I get hooked? Because it was about people and communication, people and behaviours, people and thoughts, people and beliefs, people and values… people, people, people! Finding more about myself will always peak my interest. Finding out about other people, yeah! That is great too.

Most of my adult life I have been reading books, going to seminars, taking courses, either to improve my financial situation or my self being. I have attended property courses, getting rich courses, professionally certified courses, presentation courses, communication courses, money management courses, you name it. On my professional level, all the courses that I have attended were clearly linked to each other and I could implement the level from one step to another so it all made sense. Many of the other courses that I have attended I implemented here and there though they seemed fragmented. Then, everything was brought together earlier this month (November 2015) when my eldest daughter and I had to do a business pitch and won a business competition. Every course and seminar that I had ever attended were pulled together as a whole and clicked in place. I always test and implement what I learn on courses. Some people can be hooked on courses and you see them in every course that you attend, yet they have not moved much in their life. I feel a level of under achievement if I do not implement that which I learn. Besides who wants to listen to others without knowing whether what is being said is correct or not. Once I implement or interpret it in my life, I can make up my own mind.

The more you grow the more you expand your vision. The more you question your thoughts, words and behaviours, the more you grow. Grab opportunities to grow. Sometimes these opportunities are painful and these are the ones that make you grow even further. If you are happy and comfortable in your life, why would you want to change that? You would not even want to move! When life rattles us, that is our cue to move and grow. Welcome the rattling and kiss the stick that beats you!

5. <u>Do things differently</u> – this leads nicely on from the previous point. I mentioned about the NLP (Neuro Linguistic Programming) outcome model that fascinates me. The one other thing that blows my mind is this "<u>if you always keep doing what you always do, you will always get the results that you always got</u>". I do not know where this originated from and I heard it from my

NLP trainer during one of his courses. How incredibly simple is this? Dah!!!! I would not be surprised if you have heard this before. The question is 'do you put it in practice?'. Hey even I slip. Sometimes I do and sometimes I don't. There is nothing else I need to add on this one, it is so self-explanatory.

6. <u>See for yourself</u> – do not take other people's words, thoughts and experiences for granted. Do your own test and come up with your own judgment. I have experienced starting a new job (as an example) and I am told about this manager 'be careful, he is this or that'... usually it is to do with negative traits or behaviours of that person that I need to 'watch out'. I take these with a pinch of salt. Don't get me wrong, I do not totally dismiss it; I just do my own test to get to my own judgment of the person. I am not talking here about 'judging' someone but about making my opinion of someone's character. I am different from the person who, with good intentions, is 'warning' me about that other person. How I react with others is different so, based on who I am, my experience with interacting with the person I have been warned about may be totally different from what my 'friend' has warned me about. I started a new job a couple of years ago and my direct line manager was this man who I was told is harsh, difficult, direct etc. We got on so well that I would say he is the best manager that I have ever worked with. For the duration of the time I worked there, we got on very well and complemented each other on a professional level.

The self-development books that really attract me are the ones where I can practice on myself. NLP (Neuro Linguistic Programming) attracts me for that reason too. My spiritual development is all based on being able to put things in practice. Why would I take the word of anyone and make it my own? I want to know for myself.

Also what works for someone else may not work for me because I am different.

Find things for yourself; be curious and when you have experienced it you can share it knowingly from your perspective or you can keep it all to yourself. Either way is fine.

7. Take Care of Yourself – this relates to everything about you. This would be the sum of everything – your physical aspect, the emotional, mental, spiritual, everything that is you at all levels. You are number one so look after number one. I come from a culture where we were taught to put others before us. When I came to England I brought that with me. Then, being here on my own (i.e. not having a sibling or parent nearby), juggling work, children and everything else, I realised that if I am not well, no-one else in the house can be well, when I am angry, no-one else in the house can be happy. I was the gauge of the atmosphere in the house. I was the master of ceremonies in the house. That was a big responsibility. So I learnt to take time for me so that I would be rested and relaxed. When I am not rested and relaxed I am irritable, I shout and I disturb everything around me; I am spiky. When I am not rested I cannot help anyone, I am not in a good zone to listen and advise friends and loved ones. I started switching off phones so that when I am resting I am not disturbed. Another way was to go to a hotel alone for a day or two when it was financially viable. I am referring to when my children were still young and I was building my career. Nowadays, I take a long weekend break each month in a nice hotel, ideally located remotely. Once, I remember that I did a weekend of total silence. The children had gone to their father and I stayed at home without going out and just spent my time reading a book, relaxing, cooking with no noise – no phone, no chatting, no nothing. It was bliss! Find your way of making time for you and

making a space around you so you can recharge and come back stronger.

Keep to Nature as much as possible. I am careful of what I eat and what I drink. Anything that is chemically based is not something that I want to ingest. I would look at all alternatives before I end up taking a chemical as medicine. If I have a headache or a migraine, I would try certain oil combinations as a relief. If I have a cough, I would infuse certain teas, such as ginger, turmeric, and spices as a relief. Only as a last resort would I take chemically prepared medication. I guess because my up-bringing was close to nature, I have stuck to these ways.

The same goes for my food. I cook from fresh vegetables. It is time consuming preparing fresh vegetables, and I have done it for so many years for my children but I would not compromise on this. I love food, I love nice food and I love vegetables. Keep it natural as much as possible. Nowadays, we have many gadgets that help us cut and prepare vegetables.

My grand-daughter has a peanut allergy and several food intolerances. This has turned our life upside down and forced us to give even more scrutiny to what we eat. I have adjusted my home and kitchen so that whatever I eat, she can eat too. There has been some drastic changes and the more research her Mum and I do about food allergies and intolerances, the more we realise the effect that some of our food has on us. Our quest is now to keep improving our eating style.

I am consistent about my skin as I am with my food. Keep the chemicals away and keep it 'au naturel'. I am not fussed by my skin. I do not have a problem if I have a blemish. It is what it is. I give it the moisture that it needs, usually using a cream that is not full of chemicals.

If I cannot say the word or understand the word of an ingredient, I usually stay away from it.

Food for your brain – that is also one big aspect of taking care of yourself. What do you feed your body? What do you feed your eyes? What do you feed your ears? What do you feed your brain? You choose. I believe that whatever the food you use will have an impact on your being. Is it positive or is it negative? Who knows? I am totally aware of what I want to feed myself with and I make sure that, as much as possible, that is what I get. Keep in tune with your body and listen to it. When it does not like something, take action to make it comfortable, to keep it balanced.

8. <u>Laugh and Cry</u> – I laugh and I cry a lot. I cry when I watch cartoons, I cry when I watch Indian Bollywood movies. My youngest daughter laughs at me and makes fun of me. My grand-daughter was watching me cry while watching a movie and she could not stop staring at me. She could have been thinking 'what is going on with Gammie? She has lost it!? You see, usually I do not cry of sadness but of joy and of intense emotion of love. So I could be crying and laughing at the same time. Why not?

When you want to laugh, laugh. When you want to cry, cry. As women, we can get away with crying so let's use it. When I cry, I release emotions and energy. I do not ask myself questions and over analyse. I feel like crying, I cry and then I move on. If I need to reflect on why I cried, I do so and then I move on. During my peak days when life was teaching me some harsh lessons, when the children were young and I had a challenging relationship, I would cry when life was painful. Nowadays, my crying comes from watching love movies or some inspirational clips on YouTube that are just awesome. Life does not make me cry anymore because life is great and I understand that any pain that I feel, I bring it to myself.

I do not watch movies that will make me tense. I do not watch movies that scare me. I do not watch movies that are traumatising. I watch funny movies and romantic movies. I love romance, however, I am very pragmatic about life. I am someone who practises logic and emotion a lot, therefore, I get to blend the two positively. So, if I need to feel sorry for myself, I do and then I move on. It is all about moving on, taking the next step forward. Take each moment of life as a single unit that can bring you pain or joy and, regardless of it, you need to just make the next step after that. It is not always that simple and the harder it is, the more rewarding it will be.

9. Don't do to others what you do not want done to you – this is an underlying theme of many religious beliefs. This is another axiom that is so simple and yet so profound. I have lived mainly by this all my life. I had a tenant once who had overpaid his rent. When he left there were a few pounds that should return to him and he was not at all aware of it. For a split second I thought whether I wanted to be bothered to calculate how much he had overpaid. Then, when I used that axiom, it was a no brainer.

When you are ready to betray your children, partner, friends, imagine that betrayal being done to you from them or someone else. How would you feel? How would that impact you and your life? If after taking that pause, you still go ahead with the betrayal then at least you are doing it with awareness, as a choice and not without thinking about it. If everyone was to take a pause before doing an action, the world would be a different place. I do not care whether you are a parent and it is about your child, put yourself in your child's place for a moment and reflect on how you would feel if that was being done to you. This tip continues on to the next one, so read on....

10. <u>Respect –</u> I do not partake in the 'I am your elder/parent and therefore you owe me respect regardless' rubbish. Now before you get offended by what I just wrote, this is my view, my take, my opinion and my experience. It has nothing to do with you and you have your own opinion and views and beliefs. I believe and have experienced that respect is earned – as much from a child to a parent as from a parent to a child. Your age and status do not come into play. If they do, then I call it 'pulling the hierarchy card'. What good is respect that someone gives you from fear?! Can it even be called respect?

This goes hand in hand with 'do to others what you want done to you' so give respect where it is due and it will come back to you automatically. As a mother, I have always done what I felt was right at the time and stuck with it. Did I always get it right? No. Have I given pain to my children whether consciously or unconsciously? Yes – my children would take pleasure in telling you all the stories of when I got it wrong. However, I always stuck to my decision. If it was wrong for the child, I would explain where I was coming from, why I did what I did and I would apologise, genuinely and sincerely apologise. I have apologised to all my three children at least once (I am sure many more than once). I have never regretted apologising to them because it was always about me being true to myself. Only once in my life have I done something against 'who I am' and that was with awareness to make someone feel important. This was a bitter lesson and I have never and will never ever do that again – what I mean is doing something deliberately that is against my intuition and my self-value. Sometimes it could happen unconsciously and, once I become aware of it, I would realign the situation to who I am.

But deliberately going against 'me', nope, never again. I would not do it for my children or for anyone else. I am too important in my eyes for me to allow this to happen.

Going back to the topic of respect, and anything else you want to receive back for that matter, give plenty to others and it will automatically come back to you... maybe not from the person that you gave it to in the first place but from someone else. Be open minded and aware and receive with graciousness.

Reaching Your Fulfilled Self – Your Actions

These two pages are deliberately left blank for you to note down any action you may choose to note, maybe the actions are....

- Some things that you want to keep doing because they serve you
- Some things that you want to stop doing because they do not serve you anymore
- Some new things you want to introduce in your life to expand and enrich it
- Some thoughts you want to brainstorm that you will pick up in future when you need them

Your Actions – continued...

Acknowledgements

I thank all those great teachers who have directly touched me – my parents, my sisters and brothers, my son and daughters and grand-daughter. The great men in my life, my friends, colleagues, relatives. The stranger who spurs a thought of judgment or criticism in my head and gives me the opportunity to check myself, the stranger who smiles at me and greets me. My self-development coaches and trainers, those who really look up to me and think that I am wiser and who give me the opportunity to help them unveil the wisdom they have within. Those who do not like me, those who judge me, those who do not understand me – there is really nothing to understand – those I have yet to meet, those that show me through their words and actions an example of who I do not want to become…

A lot of my teachings have been assimilated through the written words via books. I love books, I love the feel of a book, I love the mental journey that I go through that goes hand in hand with the physical journey of turning each page of a book. I thank all these teachers who have referred a book to me, gifted me with books or just pointed a book to me. I acknowledge all those indirect teachers who have written these books and who have touched me across time and space. If there was one thing I would need to take with me on a desert island, it would be a physical book!

I also acknowledge and thank everyone that has been involved in physically materialising this book from the manuscript that I produced on 26th November 2015 – my book Architect, my Editor, my Formatter, my Designer, my Foreword Authors, my Publisher.

A special acknowledgement and thanks to all those who contributed to the chapter of "How others perceive me". I did not give you much notice and it was a vague brief so thank you for taking time from your busy life to write something about me. I am honoured to have you in my life and to read about how you have experienced your interaction with me.

I deliberately do not put any names here because the list is endless and each one has had a very special and significant part into shaping me into who I am today.

Another Dedication

This book is dedicated to

Everyone that I touch
and everyone that touches me

You know Who you are!

About the Author

What else is there to add about the author? The book says a lot...

Marie-Anne is a fulfilled author, a Neuro Linguistic Programming (NLP) Practitioner, entrepreneur, mentor, professional as well as a mother and grandmother. In partnership with her daughter, Rebekha, her latest achievement is winning the award of the University of East London 10th E-Factor Entrepreneurship 2015. Marie-Anne and her daughter impressed the judges with their range of freshly baked allergy-friendly food that is targeted towards children with food allergies so that they can experience inclusion and a better quality of life when with their peers. The business idea was born from having to find creative ways to cater for the culinary needs of her grand-daughter who has a fatal peanut allergy and various food intolerances after experiencing difficulties when it came to finding appropriate food in restaurants, shops and nurseries. As always, Marie-Anne was pivotal in turning the pain and challenges of raising a child with allergies and intolerances into an opportunity. When the conventional way fails, she always looks wider than the problem for a natural way of resolving it. It comes naturally to her and she relentlessly believes that there is a way!

Marie-Anne's greatest passion is helping others empower themselves; something she has been doing intuitively for several years. She has mentored people professionally and personally to help them achieve their outcomes. Marie-Anne has a vast range of knowledge as a mother, a grand-mother, a woman, a friend and a professional. She keeps her youthful attitude by constantly improving herself. Her motivation is helping others who are willing to help themselves into taking practical steps towards their goals and reaching their highest potential. Her motto is, "If you believe in yourself, you can achieve anything."

Marie-Anne is always finding a positive angle to propel herself and others forward. She does not think like others do. In fact, she would upset some people by easily identifying the benefits that usually result out of terrible things and events. She says "If you are in the forest when a natural fire breaks, you are trapped and can only see the bad things that are happening – animals being killed, trees being destroyed... If you are above the forest and wait for a period, you will see the benefits that come out of the fire – rejuvenating earth, new and thicker growth, a recycle to better and bigger things."

Marie-Anne is a seasoned 'go-getter' and is never idle. She has travelled a long way from her native Mauritius and adopted England as her home in the early 1980s. With her children now being grown up and independent, she can finally dedicate more time to 'making waves to make a lasting improvement' in her life and others'.

Where and How to Contact me

Email
me@marie-annerase.com

Website
www.marie-annerase.com

Published Books by the Author

The Role of the Business Analyst Demystifié
(www.smartba.com)
Le rôle de l'analyste d'affaires démystifié

Future Book Coming Soon

The Beginner's Guide to Food Allergy & Intolerance
7 Topics that Everyone Should Know
(Co-authored with my daughter Rebekha Gooden)

Lightning Source UK Ltd.
Milton Keynes UK
UKOW04f0608290817
308156UK00001B/257/P